BIGFOOT UNCOVERED

Finding Sasquatch

GARY AND WENDY SWANSON

Cover image was taken by Gary Swanson on Bolan
Mountain, Josephine County, Oregon

Published by Swanson Literary Group
ISBN: 1548680591
ISBN-13: 978-1548680596

Other books by the authors:

They Saw Sasquatch
Sasquatch Encounters
Tracking Sasquatch
SASQUATCH! Reports From the Field
Bigfoot Adventures
On the Trail of Sasquatch
Sasquatch is Out There
Squatchin': Study Guide and Field Handbook for Tracking Sasquatch
Hiking Sasquatch Country: Best Hikes In Southern Oregon

Skinwalkers Shapeshifters and Native American Curses
The Last Skinwalker
We Survived Native American Witches, Curses & Skinwalkers
Skinwalker: Guardian of the Last Portal

GARY AND WENDY SWANSON

CONTENTS

INTRODUCTION

Welcome to the world of Bigfoot/Sasquatch! These sightings and encounters with this mysterious and reclusive creature are a result of our book, "Hiking Sasquatch Country."

The years we spent hiking the beautiful and rugged Southern Oregon and northernmost California areas brought us into contact with many hikers, campers, gold miners and those rugged individuals who live "off the grid!"

While also documenting our hikes with over 1,800 online photos, we met a great many people who mentioned experiences with Sasquatch, and though we had heard of the creature we had never seen one; that is until...that's another story.

Many of our readers and friends on Facebook's "Sasquatch Watch" page asked us to include some actual stories of sightings since we lived in an area that Bigfoot seemed to thrive in; so we have!

We put out the word that we would publish actual sightings and encounters and guarantee total anonymity to our submitters (if they so wished), and the stories began coming in.

We included the first submissions in "Hiking Sasquatch Country," and then for the people not interested in the hikes, but only the stories; we added a few more submissions and published "They Saw Sasquatch."

"Sasquatch Encounters" is another book of additional reports by more people who had personal stories of sightings and encounters while visiting the Pacific Northwest and from residents who were reticent about their experiences for fear of being construed as "wacky," as several submitters commented, but they still wanted to tell their story. There are also many Bigfoot stories in "Sasquatch Encounters" that happened in other Western and Midwestern states.

We have taken great care to guarantee the privacy of every submitter, and due to having proven our confidentiality, more stories have arrived and are in this third volume; "Bigfoot Uncovered."

We try to do verification of the stories we agree to accept, and although we cannot guarantee the validity of any submissions, we use due diligence to interview those whose story seems to be outside what the majority have established as the "norm;" if there could be one.

Although our personal experiences with Bigfoot are limited to only a few instances, as we are always accompanied by two curious and noisy dogs; we have interviewed enough people from all walks of life, many with highly respected credentials, that we must believe that Sasquatch lives!

In addition to thanking our contributors, we also acknowledge Dr. Don Jeffrey (Jeff) Meldrum, who is a professor of anatomy and anthropology at Idaho State University, for giving professional validity to our interest in the world of the Sasquatch. Doctor Meldrum's collection of plaster casts of Bigfoot footprints is reported to be impressive.

Unless otherwise credited, all images were provided from the files of Gary Swanson.

If you have had a personal encounter or sighting of a Sasquatch that you would like to see published in our next book, please send the details and any accompanying photos to:

swanliterary@gmail.com

If your story is published you will receive a copy of the book as our thanks.

GARY AND WENDY SWANSON

ROCKY MOUNTAIN BIGFOOT

My father recently passed away and my mother, my sister and I finally recovered enough that we were able to sit down together and go through his personal effects. We shared memories for the better part of a day, with Mom stopping periodically to tell us stories relating to certain items in Dad's collection from a lifetime of experiences.

At one point, she opened a very ancient looking box that had once held a deck of playing cards. It still had a sample card glued to the outside and it was an ace of spades. Mom picked it up with her thumb and forefinger, as one would grasp something dirty or grotesque, and she handed it to me saying, "Here Jimmy, this is more up your alley, because you like adventure like your father always did." After I took it from her, she wiped her hand on her apron, as if she had gotten it dirty from the box, even though the outsides were clean. Mom went on to caution me further, "Now if you throw it in the garbage, I wouldn't blame you one bit, but your father put such a high importance on it that I simply couldn't do it while he was still living. Just get it out of here!"

I was apprehensive as I opened the flap of the box, and inside the bulging box, wrapped in tissue, was what I first thought was a large rabbit's foot, but after removing the tissue, it looked more like a withered old toe, because it had one wide claw mark on the end that curved to a point, and on the underside, it seemed to have a pad behind the claws tip, and the other end was covered with some kind of electricians tape. Mom said, "Don't unwrap it any more while we're here, you can do it later if you want, but under the tape is bone." Now I asked, "What in the world is it from Mom? It's so big; it's like a lion's toe." She leaned back and began to explain:

When your father was stationed at Lowry Field in Denver after World War II, he was in pilot's training, and we lived off base with some of the other officers and their wives. On weekends, we liked to go up in the mountains and poke around in the old abandoned gold mines around Golden, Colorado.

We took picnic lunches along, and while we wives would poke around on the slopes and in the old abandoned rock walled cabins, the guys would explore some of the underground diggings, looking for gold and souvenirs.

Old rock walled cabin ~ CC0 Public Domain (Pxhere)

We never found much, but one day four of us went inside a long horizontal tunnel that had narrow rails for ore cars heading deep into the mountain. They didn't make good flashlights back then, so the further we went in, the dimmer it got, until we could only see a few feet in front of us; and looking back, the entrance was just a tiny speck of light. Your father and I, along with another couple were excited to continue, but the men had to keep ducking every 10 feet or so to avoid hitting their heads on the crosspieces. There wasn't a souvenir to be found, as the tunnel was absolutely litter-free!

Abandoned mine shaft ~ CC0 Public Domain (Maxpixel)

We suddenly came to a place where the water had seeped through the ceiling and frozen to almost completely block the entire tunnel except for a narrow slit about two feet wide, and almost as wide from floor to ceiling. Your dad and his buddy Don went forward to see if they could kick it hard enough to break through so we could keep on exploring, when all of a sudden, we heard a loud growl and snorting that scared us so bad that we all turned and ran as fast as we could. We thought it must be a grizzly bear still hibernating, and I think we all could imagine a large beast crashing through the ice at any moment!

Don and his wife were up ahead when we heard a thump, and Don fell down. He had smacked his head on one of the crossbeams. About a second later, your dad went crashing onto his knees from the same cause, but we were all up and running bent over, as fast as we could go! We never dared to look behind us, because we were heading toward the daylight, and with our pupils dilated, looking back it was impossible to see anything, even with flashlights, so we just kept running! The guys were moaning because of the pain from running stooped over hurt their backs, knees and sides. Finally we hit the entrance, but we didn't dare to stop, and we all ran across the open area, then climbed hand over hand up the steep, rock strewn slope on which sat the remains of an old stone walled cabin.

We were up above and about a hundred and fifty feet from the tunnel opening, and nothing had followed us. I was shaking like a leaf and my teeth were chattering from fear, but we felt pretty safe now, even if the cabin's roof was caved in, and the doors and windows were smashed. Our husbands were talking pretty brave now about rolling and throwing the large chunks of rock and concrete down on anything that came out of the mine. Each of them had tiny .25 caliber pistols in their pockets, not that they would be weapon enough for a bear, but they got more daring, because whatever it was had been afraid to come after us; maybe it couldn't get through the ice either.

They made us stay in the cabin and showed us how to climb up on the piece of roof that still remained, and to our dismay, and even threats, they climbed down and slowly approached the mine entrance again. We gals were almost in a panic and we stood ready to climb up to the roof, while your idiot father and his buddy slowly approached the entrance and then started to go in. There they were, with those silly little pistols that looked like toys; and with flashlights in hand, they started back in!

Suddenly they started firing, and Sandy and I heard a series of bangs that sounded like the guys were pulling triggers as fast as they could, and then, out they came on a dead run. Next we heard a terrible scream, which was like a high-pitched combination of mountain lion and bear. When the guys reached us and calmed us down, they said that just after they had entered the tunnel, they were met by a large shape that could have been a bear, although it was stooped over and walking on two legs and looked more ape-like. They were so shocked that they began shooting, and the creature turned and ran; and from its screams, they assumed that they must have hit it.

Finally, our brave nutcases gathered enough courage to go back one more time, because they both thought that the way the animal was limping as it ran, they may have killed it! When they came out again, my friend Sandy and I were way back up the trail where we had come from. We had enough adventure to last a lifetime. When our soldier boys finally caught up, your dad was carrying this toe. He said they found it on the ground and there was blood all around it and it trailed backed into the tunnel!

Anyway, your dad convinced his buddy that it had been his shot that made it scream, so he claimed the toe! Later on, your dad took it to a veterinarian near the Army Air Corps. Base and the doctor said it was definitely not from a bear and that it was for sure a toe, but he couldn't identify the animal species. He photographed it and circulated it among his fellows, but no one could identify the species.

Over the years I tried to get your father to throw the ugly thing away, but by then he had talked to enough people that he was convinced it was from what they called an American Yeti or Bigfoot ape back then.

My studies since my mother gave me the old card box, have me convinced that I now own a Sasquatch toe! My father went on to achieve the rank of full-bird colonel and was a well-respected man, so I would not doubt his word. Besides, it was a fun memory of my father.

T.L. ~ Colorado Springs, Colorado

ATTACK AT BRIGGS CREEK

My husband and I live in Portland, Oregon and we have plans to move to southern Oregon when we retire in a couple of years. We bought your book "Hiking Sasquatch Country" while visiting the chateau at Oregon Caves National Monument. Since we were staying in Grants Pass for two weeks, your book really came in handy. The fourth hike we followed however almost turned out to be a disaster. That's why when we saw the request on the "Sasquatch Watch" Facebook page for true stories; we decided to tell ours, because it was really something we'll never forget, and we still are kind of afraid to tell too many people, but the ones we have told all agreed that this animal is real! We believe it also, but it is hard to understand.

We took the Briggs Creek trail, because we had always had a desire to try panning for gold, and even though your book had mentioned that all of these area streams and creeks likely have registered gold claims on them, we wanted to try panning and didn't plan to keep any of the gold we found, but the thrill of finding it would be great!

With both of us nearing retirement, we want to finally start having some fun after a lifetime of pressure in our jobs. We left our car up at the parking lot, and with each of us carrying a large backpack and light sleeping bags; we planned to camp overnight as we had never before camped out under the stars.

We had wished that our dog could have made the journey with us, but he's just too old for long hikes, so he stayed with my brother in Portland.

A piece of old mining equipment along the Briggs Creek Trail

As we descended the trail, we did stop at the gravesites you indicated, and when we turned around to go back to the main path again, we heard a loud thump and a crashing back by that tall cliff that overlooks the wide clearing where the graves are.

Not seeing anything move, it would have been natural to assume that the rock just fell from the cliff and bounced toward us; however, the difference was that we had already read your story about being followed by a creature both down the valley and back up again in this same area. We weren't scared, but we were concerned; there was no reason at all for a large rock to suddenly fall from that cliff, as there had been no recent rains.

We continued down the trail and could hear the creek rushing off to our left, but as you had described, the vegetation was so thick that we couldn't even venture over to see it without getting our clothing shredded in the process, but we assumed that as wild as it was up there that it could have been anything from a coyote to a bear.

A gravesite near the Briggs Creek Trail

There was still a lot of devastation from the forest fire that burned so much of this historic and beautiful valley. Keeping in mind that your experience with being followed all happened on the trail before you crossed the creek; when we reached the place where the main route crosses the creek, we kept following the less visible trail that led down the valley, and then we had to discover the rest for ourselves.

Sap dripping from one of the large trees that burned in 2010

Basically, up until this point, we were re-living your hike, but now, as we kept descending rapidly downhill, we kept looking for a nice area where the stream was shallow and wide with a pretty area to make camp. This was the most clear and cold creek either of us had ever seen.

After going what we would estimate to be about a mile and a half further, we found the perfect spot. The creek had leveled out on a flat shelf about 25 feet long before suddenly plunging almost straight down about twenty feet into a shallow pool before continuing on its journey to join the Illinois River still far below us. We only knew it was down there, because the maps said so.

The Briggs Creek Trail

We probably would have done better to climb down to the pool below, but the climb was very steep and it was already pretty dark, because of the narrowness of the canyon and the tall trees that had escaped the forest fire. Besides, the wide upper pool where we chose to stop had a rather deep (18 inches) pool before the water plunged over the side, and we both felt that this natural lip might have captured some of the gold. In addition, this was primarily to follow your hike, and seeking gold was simply a lifelong desire on our "bucket list!"

With our machete and a collapsible army shovel we soon cleared a truly beautiful spot for our camp. We then cut some pine branches and made a crude lean-to covered with evergreen boughs to give us a feeling of security, even though it was totally open in front. It gets dark early in the forest and cold very quickly in these mountains, especially camping so close to the stream. We created a several foot circle and surrounded it with rocks, and in the center, we placed our propane stove, with the flame very low, out of respect for the beautiful forest. That night we heated beans and roasted weanies for dinner. Fortunately we had spent a lot of time practicing shorter hikes in the Mt. Hood National Forest back home, so we had the basics down pat.

Picturesque view of Briggs Creek

After nervous hours of spending our first night camping in this spooky area; the next morning we made our way to the murmuring stream and proceeded to become gold miners. It was not what we expected! After two hours of getting wet in a miserably cold mountain stream, moving what seemed like two tons of rock, and having finally found the black sand, which the people at Armadillo Mining Supply in Grants Pass said was the key to discovering gold, we actually had some fine, but absolutely gorgeous gold!

We certainly didn't find nuggets, but placed enough small flakes in our tiny bottle so that we could prove that we found gold. We felt that no one would really deprive us of the thrill of actually striking gold, so our teeny vial is now sitting on our fireplace mantel.

After we finished panning, we made it back to camp for some lunch and relaxation. We got our campfire started, and before long, the sun had set, but the most spectacular moon we had ever seen was sitting above us; it was absolutely the perfect scene!

One of the many red cedars along the Briggs Creek Trail

I don't know what time we fell asleep, but it was likely around 9:00, as with the hike in the day before, and all the activity of setting up camp and panning gold, we city slickers were exhausted.

Well, from one of the most wonderful adventures we had ever had, sometime long before midnight, things went bad! We were suddenly awakened by a huge log smashing right down on our flimsy lean-to. The only thing that kept us from being crushed was the dead tree stump alongside the lean-to. The log had fallen directly on the stump, with the other side hitting the ground, but leaving just enough room for both of us to crawl out.

Jim jumped up and turned on the flashlight; he hollered to see if I was okay, and when I weakly acknowledged being unhurt, he also turned on our fluorescent lantern. We were certain that this log could not have fallen from above, as the two trees where we had constructed our shelter had been free of dead branches when we made camp.

Now I had added my flashlight to the search and we saw nothing. No sounds, no movement, and in looking all around, we determined that this log had to have been thrown. We each took an end to move it further aside, and it had to weigh at least 80 pounds or more!

Neither of us could even consider trying to sleep. Instead, we were up and dressed, the camp stove on high, and our backup fluorescent lamp about 10 feet away to light up as much area as we could. We each had a machete, and we yelled obscenities into the darkness. The moonlight was a godsend; at least we had the benefit of enough illumination to keep us from panic!

We sat there hoping for signs of dawn, when suddenly there was a huge splash in the creek pond where we had been panning. The water even splashed some on us, and we were 25 feet away, so it must have been from a huge boulder being thrown into the pond in order for water to hit us from that far away! We yelled and threw rocks over the pond, and moved behind the trees that supported our lean-to. Suddenly, another rock of softball size bounced off our shelter trees. Not knowing what or who we were dealing with, we made the decision to pack up and leave.

Briggs Creek Trail after the 2010 fire

We moved out as best as we could, each carrying a machete and with two fluorescent lights clipped on our sides, flashlights in our other hands, we must have looked like giant fireflies as we made our way back up the trail where we had come down. It was much harder finding our way back in the dark, and just when we thought we were safe, a large dead tree branch came sailing from behind us, and we didn't hear anything until it hit Jim in the back!

Jim grunted aloud and fell to his knees, and as I turned, both of my lights hit our back-trail, and there stood a large, brownish-black animal that looked like an ugly, bearded giant, except that its eyes had a reddish glow in the moonlight; no skin showed on its face or hands, only long fur! I could see enough of it to tell that its feet were huge. In retrospect, it had to be around nine feet tall, and I remember screaming something like, "Go way and leave us alone you #$@&%*!," and it turned and disappeared down the trail. I guess it wasn't used to being cursed at.

Anyway, I helped Jim to his feet; he wasn't broken or cut, just painfully bruised. By now we were about 20 feet from that place where the main trail crosses the creek, so now we were able to make better time due to such a well-used and wider path. It took us about two hours to get down to this point, and 40 minutes to get back to the car. I'll never forget the putrid, rotten odor of this creature; it smelled like rotting meat! We now own a handgun and it goes on all of our hikes, but as Jim said, "I wouldn't even dare to shoot that big monster!"

Tammy S. ~ Portland, Oregon

KEEPER OF THE GRAVES

Our story goes way back to a trip we made to Oregon in 1980. My husband Tom and I were living in Redding, California, and we used to spend our vacations in Southern Oregon, and now that Tom has retired, we moved to Eugene, Oregon where our daughter lives. She is the one who gave us your Sasquatch book and she mentioned your request for anyone who has a true story to tell to send it to you. Please consider our experience for your new book.

This happened, as I mentioned, in July of 1980. We were doing research on old military forts, which has been an ongoing interest of ours. Even though it wasn't much of a fort, we thought as long as we were vacationing in Oregon, we'd look for Camp Watson over by Mitchell in Wheeler County, Oregon.

As we traveled the area, we had the pleasure of watching a beautiful pair of golden eagles, the first we had ever seen, as they played at diving at each other in a large meadow between two buttes. At first there was quite a bit of RV traffic, probably folks on their way to *The Painted Hills* or the *John Day Fossil Beds,* but it wasn't too long before we were the only ones on this particular road.

Anyway, we were looking for a place where there were supposed to be seven soldier's graves at a location where you had to cross an old sawmill property; the instructions we were given said you needed to close the gate behind you, however when we finally found the gate, it was padlocked and chained. We stopped at a neighboring property, and the people were very nice, they said the gate hadn't been locked before, but the owner was out of town, so that was maybe the reason for the padlock.

When they found out that we were just exploring, they did tell us a little about the historic townsite of Antone. The property then belonged to an Oldsmobile dealer in California, but they pointed out a road that would take us to the cemetery, as it was about the only indicator that any people had once lived here.

We had to cross a couple of properties on the dirt trail (basically two ruts), but it was dry and we'd go through a wobbly, barbed-wire gate, close it behind us, then through another with the same procedure, and suddenly we were on a knoll overlooking the vast hills and valleys over what seemed an expansive, uninhabited area, except we were sure it was cattle country, as we had spotted small groups of cows and calves numerous times. We parked near the small, wrought iron fenced cemetery and were amazed by the large number of gravestones that told a sad story of so many children who had died; they were anywhere from a month or two old to six years. So terribly many had died within days of their birth; it was simply heartbreaking! Such a desperate life these brave pioneers must have faced as they fought to settle this wild, new country.

Walking down a winding dirt trail toward the deep valley, we saw evidence where this had obviously been an area where gold dredges had been there in force. Large areas of rock mounds alongside the creek indicated that a gold dredge had floated its way along the meandering waterway, picking out the gold and leaving a snake-like trail of rocks and boulders bordering the entire length as far as the eye could follow. These dredges created their own huge lakes to float on as they took out the gold and left the rocks and dirt in their wake.

Gold dredge in Sumpter Valley, Oregon
By Doug from Portland, USA (Pardon me) [CC BY 2.0
(http://creativecommons.org/licenses/by/2.0)], via Wikimedia Commons

At the bottom of this otherwise deserted series of hills was a two-story home, obviously from pioneer times; it had a cupola on the top that almost resembled a bell tower, but we thought that it also would have come in handy as a lookout during the Oregon Indian wars. We labored our way along the old road that was rutted from storms and stumbled over loose gravel down the steep slope. Making our way up to the house, we noted that there were no remaining windows or doors; however, there was no apparent damage from rain or snow. It was apparent someone had lived here well beyond the pioneers, because there were newspapers glued to all of the walls obviously for insulation purposes.

I remember one large ad that announced Pontiac's new 8-cylinder engine in a large ad, but it was too high on the wall to read the date; I know it was old. Even with no window glass, the newspapers were legible and everything was clean and dry. There was no discernable means to reach the upper story, but it was visible from a hole in the living room ceiling, so they must have used a long ladder. We became more interested in the old-time pile of bottles and cans by the creek that ran nearby, as the ancient bottle dumps can hold rare treasures. So off we went, but all we found were gigantic piles of broken glass that had succumbed to ages of target shooters. Too many looters had preceded us!

We were about to explore further, when all of a sudden, our car horn started blaring; and looking up toward the cemetery, we saw what looked to be a big, tall bear standing on its hind legs. It was thinner than bears we had seen before, and it was excitedly beating at the car, but still on two feet! Next, as we were running up the hill, slipping on loose gravel, stumbling and quickly running out of breath, the creature picked up a large rock. We thought maybe then it might be just a human in costume, because bears can't do that; then it turned and smashed out our rear side window, and reached in and pulled out a shopping bag that we had full of the goodies that normally accompany us on outings. There were some sandwiches, cookies, a couple of fruit pies, candy and nuts.

We had almost reached the hilltop, and by now, we could barely walk from the severe exertion; Tom slipped and fell, and I looked to see if he was alright, and when I looked back up, the Bigfoot animal was way past the cemetery and on its way into a stand of pine trees. Judging from how big it looked, we were glad that it ran away!

Looking back on this experience, we truly believe that the Sasquatch does exist! To further add credibility and ease our previously doubtful minds, on the way out we stopped back at the home where the lady had given us directions, and as she listened to our story, her head was slightly nodding, and then she said, "Oh, so you got to meet our *keeper of the graves.*" She said they call him that because he's seldom ever seen except he seems to watch over the pioneers, but he'd never done any damage before. She thought he must be hungry and said she would leave some eggs and potatoes out for him. She went on to say he has a way of smelling food, because she puts it up high on a garage window sill so the deer can't reach it and he seems to know it's for him and never does any damage around the place. With that, she didn't wish to speak further, so we told her we'd not speak of it.

This all happened long ago, so please consider our story if you publish a new book. It really was an experience neither of us will ever forget!

Jackie A. ~ Eugene, Oregon

GOLD MINING WITH SASQUATCH

I heard about your book from a neighbor, so if you are still looking for true Bigfoot encounters, this actually happened to me back in 1971. The memory is so vivid; I remember every bit of it! I never told many people about it, because it seems that in Oregon such experiences are normal.

I had been out in the area of Steamboat Springs east of Roseburg, Oregon and I was going in the dense forests to target practice with a new revolver I had just purchased.

I packed up to leave after sighting in, and I stopped when I got back to the main cutoff leading to the highway, and there sat an old Ford "Woody" station wagon. There was an elderly gentleman standing beside it, so I stopped to see if he needed help. Well, that was the beginning of a good friendship and an experience I'll never forget!

This man's name was Al Renfro*; we stood and talked for over an hour, and it all started when I noticed that the entire back seat of his station wagon was full of textbooks. They seemed so out of place with the shovels, picks, hammers and other tools that were in there; I had to know! It turned out Al was 85 years old, and his wife had passed away a couple of years before, and being distraught, he gave his Klamath Falls, Oregon home to his adult children and became a gold miner.

He filed a claim in the Umpqua National Forest and he moved into the woods.

Forest trail in the Umpqua National Forest ~ By Jsayre64 (Own work) [CC BY-SA 3.0 (http://creativecommons.org/licenses/by-sa/3.0)], via Wikimedia Commons

Al made enough money mining that in the summer he mined gold and in the winter he attended the University of California in Berkley. He was about a year from earning his degree in geology at that time. He said he had already had a good career, but geology had been a lifelong hobby.

We struck up such a quick friendship that he gave me directions to his mine, and a week later, I showed up for his invitation to visit. His directions led me deep in the forest on a road that was little more than a trail, and I parked in a spot where there were several other vehicles that appeared to have been there a while, as they were all dusty. This was the end of the trail.

I parked and set out walking the well-worn path along this creek when all of a sudden; a woman stepped out of the bushes holding a shotgun and aggressively demanded to know what I wanted. I told her I was on the way to see Al Renfro, and she immediately softened and apologized for her gruffness; explaining how there were several gold claims on the creek and they had to constantly be on guard against trespassers. Although it is legal to walk across a gold claim as long as you don't pick up anything, I sure wouldn't have wanted to challenge this gal's claim! She said, "I'll take you to his claim, follow me." So I did, and on the way, I saw several more people from a distance that noticed us, and then waved in recognition as my guide signaled to them. When we got to Al's claim, as soon as he recognized me, my armed escort turned without a word and with a quick nod to Al, she was gone.

Well, I was really in for a surprise when Al showed me around! There above the creek on a small knoll, sat a huge wooden A-frame; it was monstrous! It must have been at least 25 feet wide and it rose above me over 20 feet at the peak. There was a main plank floor with a loft above, accessed by a set of wooden stairs. Al introduced me to a young hippie couple that he shared this A-frame with; they had partnered with Al to help share the working of the claim. They seemed like the San Francisco "flower children" I had watched on T.V.

They had both a placer claim and a hard rock claim on the creek; this was a tributary of Steamboat Creek. They had a large pit with a triangular set of poles high overhead and pulleys down into the open mine. They would fill buckets with gravel and hoist them up, and then carry them to the adjacent stream to sluice out the gold. In addition to that, while two people worked to bring up the gold from the hard rock claim, the third would be running the dirt from the stream through another sluice box nearby.

North Umpqua near the mouth of Steamboat Creek
By Donaleen (http://creativecommons.org/licenses/by/2.0)], via
Wikimedia Commons

Judging from the lumber that the A-frame was built with, I was curious to know just how much money they could be making out here in the wilderness, but of course out of courtesy, I didn't ask.

When we returned from touring the operation, Al took me into the A-frame, which for as nicely built as it was, had only three sides; it was open in the front. The roof was built to overhang the open wall, and the way it sat down in this valley, with the huge trees towering above it, it was cozy. Along the entire back wall was a long, deep counter. It was above waist high and would have been a beautiful workshop. There were drawers below it and kitchen-like cabinets above; all done out of pine.

Al beckoned me over to the counter and said, "Now I'll show you the reason for all of the secrecy and why we all carry guns." With that, he pulled open several of the massive drawers, and I could not believe my eyes. There, laying in rows, were glass test tubes full of gleaming gold; row upon row of pure gold! The tubes were several layers deep, and stacked on top of each other in the heavily constructed drawers. Each drawer must have been 12 inches by 20 inches and about 10 inches deep I was flabbergasted! No wonder he and his companions could spend winters in California. This beautiful gift from nature was not only paying for his college education, it was providing a great living for all of them. Al explained that they sold most of the gold on the black market in San Francisco, because it paid over double to four times the other markets; especially for the nuggets that were able to be set into jewelry. They were worth many times their weight.

I had brought my sleeping bag and a cache of goodies, including a few "extras," so later after we all ate, I settled into my corner of the downstairs under the watchful eye of Al's old yellow lab.

Along about two o'clock in the morning, I was awakened by the sound of a splashing in the creek, and I dismissed it as being a deer or bear. Since I was awake, I decided to take a trip to the outdoor nature's latrine. I had brought a small flashlight, and since the moon was bright enough, I waited until I was a ways away from the A-frame, at a wide shelf alongside the water before turning my flashlight on.

The minute the light came on; I heard a loud grunt followed by the sound of some large animal crashing through the thick brush just down from where I was stopped. I shined the light down and to my right where the noises were coming from expecting to full-well see a bear, like Al said he had killed there the week before; when this huge nine or 10 foot creature went tearing down the path ahead, and it was on its hind legs! All I could think of at the moment was King Kong; the beast was huge! Why it ran from me I don't know, because it looked like it was double my size. All I could think of to do was to just keep shining my light in the direction it had run; more to make sure it kept going than anything else.

After a few minutes, I carefully retreated to the safety of the A-frame; having serious misgivings about the open front. The next morning I told everyone about my experience, and they all nodded their understanding, without any surprise; and they said almost in unison, "We should have warned you about that possibility, but he hasn't been around for months, so we forgot." No alarm, no worry, just a casual understanding that this animal lived out there and they all shared the remote, beautiful forest. They didn't seem to want to discuss it further, so I just let it drop.

I had all but forgotten about that incident, as I heard from a friend at the forestry office that Al had passed away not too many years after that, about the time the government closed the area to mining in order to protect the trout spawning streams. Strange how they always use that reason, or something similar, to close our forests to most activities.

T. Snow ~ Myrtle Creek, Oregon

* *Publisher's note: This gold claim under Al Renfro's name from Klamath Falls, Oregon has been verified by the government mining records in Portland, Oregon. We researched it since the mine owner's name was mentioned. The state forestry department knew Mr. Renfro well, and they sounded like they had a genuine respect for this gentleman according to the ranger we interviewed.*

ENCOUNTER AT THE RIVER OF NO RETURN

As per our telephone conversation, I am enclosing the agreed upon Sasquatch event that took place near the Frank Church River of No Return Wilderness area in Idaho. Let's just say that at the time this occurred, I was in law enforcement, and let it go at that. Even though this happened years ago, I still have a concern over a conflict of interest if my name was disclosed as this event is only partially a part of the public record.

The town of Yellow Pine is where this began. I traveled northeast of Yellow Pine to the town of Big Creek, and there I met with a landowner who had asked for "non-official" help, and we headed due east along Big Creek. I will only tell you that this man owned a place up there, and he had filed a complaint with my department that his dogs kept disappearing, and he also had a calf killed and partially eaten. This sort of a thing happens in these very remote areas, but the dangers of a rogue bear or wolves that begin killing domestic animals, and getting too familiar with civilization, we take seriously. Oftentimes these types of occurrences, although partially recorded to account for time spent, are necessarily obscured to the full events that took place to protect those involved.

I left my department's 4-wheel drive pickup at the landowner's home and we got aboard his backwoods crawler, and off we went through the woods along a well-used animal and snowmobile route, that this time of year, made a good, brushless trail. The woods were fairly dry, so we made pretty good time to the man's back forty, and then we left his rig there and took our packs and headed up and away from Big Creek. We must have been close to the edge of the Payette National Forest when we stopped for the night. We prepared a camp site and then (let's call him Walt) Walt showed me the first kill.

A young heifer lay in a well matted down grassy spot, and Walt said the killer had obviously returned to feed several more times since he first discovered the kill. The cow was getting very ripe, so we returned to camp and fashioned a quick lean-to and covered it with pine boughs; we were fairly well sheltered from the cold, and before sunset we cut a supply of firewood from a lightning-killed oak tree that lay beside the creek.

By this time, two of Walt's large dogs that had wandered off exploring, caught up with us and roamed the area until we ate. Walt cut off some chunks of the dead cow and cooked them over the fire for the dogs; while we stuck with our sandwiches and a couple of franks we had in the cooler. Several times during the night the dogs growled and took off out of camp and we could hear them barking far off; something had them rattled.

We awakened early the next day, and even though we had each taken turns at feeding our fire during the night, it was cold and dead. I thought we'd freeze to death before we got a blaze going, but finally we did, and must have sat there for an hour just getting warm and drinking coffee. A thin coating of ice had formed on the slower moving side of the creek, and strangely, the dogs were nowhere to be seen, but their tracks showed where they had apparently been all around on the banks of the creek. Walt whistled and called, but they didn't show up.

We broke camp and set out on foot to where Walt said he had followed these large tracks that led away from his cow, and there were signs of the dogs' fresh prints in the dirt along the creek, so we decided to follow their trail. The tracks followed the creek bed, and suddenly we found some prints that looked almost human, but very large. Walt pointed out that the monster-sized footprints had obliterated the dog prints, and since he is a professional hunter and woodsman, I accepted his theory that whatever this was had walked on the trail of the dogs, but after they had been there! This was kind of unnerving, and since I've been in this line of work, I've seen a lot of things, but the size of these footprints made me glad I had a gun!

We followed the tracks for about a quarter mile and then the damndest thing happened; all of a sudden this big, shaggy looking, bear-like animal broke out of some small fir trees along the creek bank and ran up the hill to our left. It looked like a thin grizzly bear, but it was running on its hind legs and it didn't have a snout. It had an almost wolf-like face with short ears and long, shaggy arms covered with brownish hair.

We chased after it and it ran up a shallow wash, then up a brush covered ravine, and as we ran after it, it kept gaining on us and it seemed to just run through the brush and trees with hardly a sound. We must have followed it for over a mile, and it seemed to know those thick forests very well. I became disoriented until we broke out on a ridge above what had to be Big Creek. I had not been in this remote area before, so I was just following my gut instincts.

Big Creek Bridge in the Frank Church-River of No Return Wilderness
By Rex Parker (Big Creek Bridge) [CC BY 2.0
(http://creativecommons.org/licenses/by/2.0)], via Wikimedia Commons

I was on a ridge looking down about a hundred feet and Walt ended up along the same cliff, only about two hundred feet from me. As we gave each other an acknowledgement, all of a sudden in the trees between us, was the creature we had been chasing! In the excitement of the pursuit, I became overcome with the feeling that this was some sort of a felon I was after, and I yelled, "Get down Walt," and drew my 44 magnum revolver from its holster and took aim at the creature's chest and pulled the trigger! The animal sprang up, and with a shriek, it either jumped off or fell off the cliff and down into the brush and heavy vegetation that clung to the sides of the cliff.

Both Walt and I searched for blood sign and any evidence that I had hit the animal, but we found only a fairly large patch of hair, but no blood. We tried to find a way down the cliff, but it was so steep that we figured we would have to go about a mile downstream to where the bank finally got down to running alongside the creek again, and since it was now about noon, we decided to call it quits and go look for the dogs and then return to Walt's place. My department would not have appreciated having to form a search and rescue, as I had checked out for a maximum of four days; that is the longest time for one agent to be out of contact on a citizen request for assistance.

It was getting toward mid-afternoon when we finally neared our camping spot and we were about a half mile from the camp when we came upon Walt's dogs. They were lying in the tall grass near the creek, and they had literally been torn to pieces! Walt broke down in tears, and I went back to camp and retrieved my camp shovel and buried them together on the Creekside under a pretty willow tree. I could feel Walt's sorrow, as I know they were like his children.

We silently broke camp and returned to Walt's home with the sad news for his family. Walt and I agreed to never speak of this incident, but I have always lived with the guilt that I, as a government official, had likely murdered an innocent animal that was just being as it was created, and living by its means. I have also been plagued by the fact that if this was one of these Sasquatch beasts, it may have been worth the effort to search further, but I can imagine the reaction from my hard-nosed supervisor to a request for agents to hunt for a "killer ape-man!"

Cabin Creek in the Frank Church-River of No Return Wilderness
By Rex Parker (Cabin Creek) [CC BY 2.0
(http://creativecommons.org/licenses/by/2.0)], via Wikimedia Commons

I'm telling you this story as a way of getting it off my conscience, at the urging from my wife, as she said I've been remorseful over it for 14 years now since I retired. We heard about your request for Sasquatch incidents from a friend, and as I had taken him into my confidence a few years ago on a fishing trip, he said maybe it was time. My wife said, "You're such a lousy shot, you probably missed it anyway." I just wish I really knew.

Anonymous ~ Ketchum, Idaho

SASQUATCH RESCUED ME

In the summer of 2012 I read the book "Lost" by Cheryl Strayed; as you know, it was about her experiences hiking the Pacific Coast Trail by herself. At the time, I thought, "What a gutsy woman!" About 18 months later, I felt rather lost myself. My husband suddenly and unexpectedly died from a brain aneurism. This left me alone to run our law practice; but I was making a mess of things. My thoughts turned back to Ms. Strayed's journey on the P.C.T. and I began thinking that if I were to do something similar it just might be the cathartic help I needed to heal.

Early in 2014 I began making my own plans to hike the Pacific Coast Trail, but not all of it; I decided I would only do the Oregon portion starting from the Columbia River and heading south. I determined if I started on July 1st I could reach Ashland by August 15th. As an anticipated reward, I made reservations at the Lithia Springs Resort where I would spend a week relaxing after my journey's end before flying back to Portland.

I had a friend drop me off at the Cascade Locks access to the trail, and off I went. There were fewer people on the trail than I thought there would be, and I have to admit, it's rather frightening when the sun goes down and you are all alone. Most of the people I met were hiking north, except for a few groups that I talked to in various resupply points. By the time I reached Mazama Village at Crater Lake on July 25th, I had traveled about 325 miles on foot and thousands emotionally. I was starting to feel stronger and more optimistic about what my future held.

Views from Cascade-Siskiyou National Monument
By Bureau of Land Management Oregon and Washington [CC BY 2.0 (http://creativecommons.org/licenses/by/2.0) or Public domain],
via Wikimedia Commons

On the 27th I headed towards Callahan's Lodge. I calculated I should reach it in about six or seven days, as it was 104 miles away. I looked forward to spending a night there before I arrived at the Lithia Springs Resort.

I had been back on the trail for three days when my nightmare started. Two guys overtook me late that afternoon. They said hello and went on their way. That night I found a nice spot off the trail to spend the night and went about setting up camp. I had just got my tent set up when I looked up to find the same two men that passed me a few hours ago standing in my camp area watching me.

Instinctively I knew I was in trouble, then one of them pulled his knife out of a scabbard he had on his belt and started coming toward me. I started screaming and threw my camp shovel at him before I began running. I was overcome by panic and was running without any idea of where I was going. I tripped and fell over some large rocks and started stumbling down the side of a steep hill. When I landed, dazed and confused, I could hear some terrible noises from my camp. It sounded like someone was being torn up by a bear or wolves!

After the fall, I could see I had many scrapes and cuts, and some were bleeding profusely. I slowly got up, and thank goodness nothing was broken. I made my way to a stand of trees. I sat down there and realized the noises from above had stopped, but I heard something coming down the hill to where I was. I hid myself in the trees as well as I could, but whoever or whatever was still heading in my direction.

I looked up and standing there looking at me was the biggest man-beast I have ever seen. It was covered with a dark brownish orange fur and had to be over seven feet tall. It had huge hands and the feet were even larger. It bent down to look at me, and suddenly it picked me up, threw me over its shoulder and carried me away. By now I was petrified and sobbing, but I knew I didn't have a chance to get away. It smelled pretty rank, like I would expect a bear to smell.

The creature finally set me down. I could see we were in a

cave and I could hear water running nearby. It started looking closely at my wounds and then it stood up and went back farther into the cave. When it came back it had some moss in its hands/paws, and it sat down and began to chew on the moss. It began to apply the chewed up moss to my cuts. When it was apparently satisfied with the job, it looked into my eyes.

I was so surprised by the intelligence I saw there! It was looking at me as though it was worried about me and wasn't sure how to treat me. It lifted up one of those big, meaty hands and began to stroke my head; like you would pet a dog.

The creature had streaks of blood in its fur and I wasn't sure whether it was from my wounds or from whatever had taken place at my campsite.

By now I realized this was a Sasquatch and he wasn't going to harm me! I think he was quite old; the hair around his lips and ears was white, and his hands were gnarled as if he had arthritis.

At some point I must have fallen asleep, because when I next looked around, it was daylight outside of the cave, my body was covered with branches from a fir tree and my rescuer was gone. I hobbled towards the sound of the running water and found a small stream running through one side of the cave. After slaking my thirst, I realized how cold I was and went outside the cave to look for something to burn.

I was gathering twigs when my Sasquatch returned. He had some kind of pack, it looked to be made of small branches, and it was full of blackberries. I followed him back into the cave; those blackberries were the best I have ever tasted. After we finished our meal, I piled up the twigs I had gathered along with a few leaves. When I reached into my pocket and brought out my disposable lighter and put it to the sticks and lighted them, Mr. Sasquatch was terrified. He growled and ran away just as fast as he could. I hadn't stopped to think about how fire would have frightened him.

While he was gone, I took the opportunity to wash off my scrapes and cuts in the stream and spent the rest of the day recuperating. When the Sasquatch finally came back, he had my backpack with him. My bedroll was still attached and all my supplies were still inside.

That night I got out two of the MREs I had with me and some beef jerky. Sasquatch seemed to enjoy the meal, but he turned down the beef jerky. I think perhaps Sasquatch could be vegetarian. We sat for awhile in companionable silence before the Sasquatch left again. I spent the night in my bedroll near the small fire I built, and awoke early as the sky was just beginning to lighten. Sasquatch again came with berries; I'm not sure what kind they were, although they looked like large blueberries. After we ate, I knew I needed to get on my way. My cuts were healing well and I felt ready to continue.

I looked at my Sasquatch and he looked so sad; he must have known I was getting ready to leave. I think he must have been lonely and enjoyed my companionship. He again petted my head and gave a big sigh. I stood up and put my pack on, took a deep breath and gave the Sasquatch a quick hug.

We walked outside the cave and he pointed to a trail that wound back up to the PCT. I was back up there in no time at all and when I turned to look back toward the cave, he was still standing there watching. I waved and then started on my way. I thought about returning to my old campsite to see if I could determine what had taken place there, but I decided to leave it alone and put it out of my mind.

It took me three days to get to Callahan's Lodge, and although I wonder what happened to the two men that tried to hurt me, I didn't say anything to anyone about it. I cancelled my reservation in Ashland and stayed at Callahan's for a couple of days before arranging transportation to Medford so I could fly home.

I've never told this story to anyone. The Sasquatch I met saved my life, and I don't want anyone to try to seek them out; I know it would only be disastrous to their kind.

Sally A. ~ Portland, Oregon

BIGFOOT'S FIRST HUNT

My wife and I moved to Medford, Oregon last year from Stillwater, Minnesota and have pretty much been hiking and exploring this gorgeous country ever since.

We were shown your Sasquatch Watch Facebook page by friends with whom we shared a very frightening experience.

We had already been on several hikes along the Rogue River, and we drove all the way down to the townsite, or whatever they call Marial*, Oregon. That road was really long and pothole riddled, but we left our car at the Marial Lodge and spent two days hiking downriver and then returned to spend the night at the lodge.

The next morning we headed back up river but as we were making dust back toward home, we came upon a small child, who from a distance appeared to be all covered in a camouflage outfit of brown, and it was dragging a small animal that looked like a deer. The place it had crossed led off to our left, and when we got up to where it went, there was a narrow road that was more like a path with grass growing in the middle. We both agreed that we simply had to know what was happening, so out of curiosity, we turned down this road and I drove a little faster to see if I could catch up to the kid and see what kind of animal he had as it wasn't hunting season and even so, the deer was too young.

We bounced along as the narrow road curved to the left, and suddenly, there they were!

Right where the narrow road started up a hill, the boy had left the road, and that's when we got the shock of our lives! It wasn't even human, and the thing was about four feet high and looked like a skinny baby ape. My wife screamed at me to stop, and I hit the brakes just as a large, ape-like giant appeared from the bushes, grabbed the smaller one by the arm, and jerked it and the deer it was still hanging on to into the air, and within two seconds they were gone!

As we sat there in shocked silence, collecting our thoughts, we finally were able to speak. We agreed that the adult must have been at least seven or eight feet tall, because I stood by the place we had last seen them, and Jenny said it seemed two heads taller than my 5'11". We were, strangely enough, not frightened, as they were obviously more afraid of us; so we got back in the car and slowly drove up the sandy road, and there on the top of the rather large, flat area was an old cemetery.

We quietly walked around the graveyard and after a few minutes, we headed back toward our car when all of a sudden a piece of rotted log sailed out of nowhere and landed right in front of us. We both yelled, out of a combination of fear and anger, and then another larger piece of tree limb came crashing down, so needless to say, we felt quite unwelcome and we left in a hurry.

Rafters on the Rogue River near the Marial Lodge

We decided to return to the lodge to report the incident, as there is a government building there which appeared to be like a ranger station that is only occasionally occupied, and there happened to be someone there with two local year-round residents. Our story was met with interest and a few nodding heads, but evidently this happens infrequently, so no one was alarmed. The folks at the lodge told us that there was a family of the Bigfoot animals that lived in the area, but they never really did any damage, so they said they don't advertise it because it may scare away business. On the flip-side, the owners said if word got out, they'd get the undesirable visitors called "Sasquatch hunters." That, we don't need!

Dennis S. ~ Medford, Oregon

* *Publisher's note: We have a friend who had a schoolmate whose father owned several gold mines in that area, and Dave said they used to go up to the mines when they were teenagers and set off dynamite charges.*

The town of Marial was named after Marial Billingsley, and our friend's schoolmate was a Billingsley. The property was named after Marial Billingsley when she was a young girl, and has remained in the family ever since.

The Billingsley's and the others who settled this area, called the "Rogue River Canyon" were white gold miners and their Native American wives. After the gold fields on the Klamath River in California began to play out in the 1850s, these folks moved into this remote and rugged canyon in not only their search for gold, but also to farm and raise their families. This entire canyon is still occupied by descendants of these hardy pioneers.

GHOST TOWN GUARDIAN

My wife and I moved to Pendleton, Oregon from Great Falls, Montana to help her aging parents and manage their ranch property.

We have enjoyed many excursions to explore Oregon's exciting past. One most memorable trip was when in our travel trailer staying at a campground in Baker City. Our travels took us to gold mines, and to valleys that had been totally dug up by huge gold dredges, and the large gold mining operations with their massive buildings standing guard all throughout these mountains.

We spent time at the county offices in Baker City, and met by chance, an old pioneer who had been a gold miner for many years. He told us that the first county seat was the town of Auburn. We spent a very enjoyable hour over lunch while our new friend regaled us with stories of the early times in the area.

We spent time at the county offices in Baker City, and met by chance, an old pioneer who had been a gold miner for many years. He told us that the first county seat was the town of Auburn. We spent a very enjoyable hour over lunch while our new friend regaled us with stories of the early times in the area.

Baker City Hall - built in 1903
By Visitor7 (Own work) [CC BY-SA 3.0
(http://creativecommons.org/licenses/by-sa/3.0)], via Wikimedia Commons

We spent time at the county offices in Baker City, and met by chance, an old pioneer who had been a gold miner for many years. He told us that the first county seat was the town of Auburn. We spent a very enjoyable hour over lunch while our new friend regaled us with stories of the early times in the area.

Mr. Henry, our new friend, gave us directions to the area where the town of Auburn sat. Early the next morning we made our way to what at one time was a city of six to eight thousand miners, although there is absolutely no trace of it ever having had any occupants! We truly had a tough time finding it. Parking at the edge of a dirt road that appeared to have little use, we made our way into a rocky valley that was beneath a couple of large manmade ponds that had been a major source of water for sluicing the grounds in this vast valley.

We got there after some recent spring rains, so there were large places that had newly been eroded from the rains, and as we walked the area that looked like a huge gravel pit, we found some broken pieces of Chinese opium pipes and shards of porcelain, but nothing of value.

The history of this typical boom town was that this entire city had been composed of hastily built buildings, gambling dens, miner's supply stores and saloons scattered all around the area. The miners lived in anything from shacks to lean-tos to tents.

Later, after the gold production was waning, a wildfire burned the entire city to the ground. Next, as so often happened back then, the white miners moved on and the Chinese moved in. Our new friend, Mr. Henry, had informed us that everyone thought this area had been cursed, because the next disaster that ultimately ended the town of Auburn's existence was a tremendous flood. As the fire had destroyed all the trees, there was nothing to stabilize the soil and everything was utterly devastated, and even the super patient and determined Chinese miners up and left.

The only thing that survived in this area was a partial corral and building that may have belonged to a hostler. On the corner post was nailed an extremely rusted and large horseshoe. It was nailed open-end up, so according to superstition, the luck was still in it. It was solidly held in place by ancient nails. We could not resist, and even though we weren't supposed to, this lucky horse shoe now has a nice home with us; we firmly believe it saved us from harm just about an hour later!

We stopped for lunch at what had been a wagon road between two ramps that had been used for driving a large freight wagon in and loading it from the ramps; we were admiring the ingenuity of these miners when a rock about football-sized suddenly smashed into our thermos. With coffee and sandwiches flying in all directions, we instinctively ducked and circled to look for the cause, but we were alone! We were in a sort of bowl, and it was over two hundred feet to the nearest cliff. Knowing it was impossible for this to have been an accident; we took the hint, grabbed our broken equipment and knapsack and headed back toward where we came in.

I yelled a couple of times, more to let whoever did it know that I was mad, than anything else, but we were both trying to figure if it was kids with a catapult or what. Suddenly behind us a shaggy form appeared at the place where we had picnicked, and it was shaking and stomping its feet and making sounds like loud, hoarse coughing and snorting! Then it must have thought we weren't leaving fast enough, because it lobbed another rock at us; and I swear we were over two hundred feet away, and this rock the size of a salad bowl flew over our heads and was close enough to make us both duck.

The animal was covered with long, brown, shaggy fur, and when it appeared first at the spot we had been eating, it was in the trench between the two ramps, and it was taller than the top of the ramps which I'm sure means it was over seven feet tall!

I almost threw the horseshoe away in my haste to quickly grab our stuff, but my wife reminded me that we were not hurt, so we agreed that it was really lucky. We stopped in at a small grocery store in Baker and the friendly storekeeper listened to our story with a nod and a knowing grin, and he just said, "I see he's still with us; thought he'd moved on, but that critter has been out there for years." Then he gave us our change and simply went back to his work like it was no surprise!

image by Ben L. ~ Pendleton, OR

Since that happened, we have heard of similar instances in Eastern Oregon from acquaintances, and it was an experience we have told over and over every time someone inquiries about our old, rusted horseshoe.

Ben L. ~ Pendleton, Oregon

COLLIDING WITH BIGFOOT

I was running late because I stopped off for a couple of beers after working a 10 hour shift at the mill in Roseburg. It was about 9:00 p.m. and there was almost no traffic on our loop road, as there were only a half a dozen houses on this lonely stretch of narrow paved road.

As I crossed over the bridge spanning our small creek, I braked slightly to prepare for the bump where the paving had sunk below the concrete bridge, and once I crossed the span, I prepared to increase my speed as I reached the other side when suddenly there was a body in front of my car! I dynamited the brakes thinking it was a neighbor's kid; and as my tires screeched, my headlights shone on a human looking being, but it was an animal.

It had a human looking body, but all covered in hair. At the second before my swerving car hit the animal, a huge being darted in front of the car and in one flash, it whisked up the little one. Fortunately, when I slammed on the brakes, my car's rear end had swung out to the left and as it lurched to a stop, the left door hit the bigger of the hairy apes and sent them both sprawling down the bank into the ditch.

I was shaking, but I pulled forward to the side of the road, and leaving my lights on; I grabbed my flashlight and stumbled across the road to see what I had hit. I shined my light down into the ditch, but there was nothing there. Then I moved the beam to where the hill started to climb steeply, and there was what looked like a long armed bear, but it was running on its hind legs and it had the youngster over its right shoulder and it seemed to be limping. When my powerful light hit the animals, the big one started hobbling faster, and even from a distance, I could see that they weren't bears. The little one was looking at me, and its face didn't have a long nose; it seemed more like a chimpanzee, and its eyes reflected an almost red color. By then they were probably a 100 feet away and disappeared into the trees.

When I got home, I pulled into the garage and turned on the overhead lights. My wife came out to see what I was doing, and I told her about it as we both examined the car. The only place it was damaged was on the driver's door where it was dented and the chrome molding was sticking out at an angle. That was when Angie pulled a gob of long brown hair from under where the molding was bent. I knew my insurance company would think I had been drinking if I told them what I really hit, so I reported it as a deer.

My wife's father works for the U.S. Fish and Wildlife department in another state, so on the off-chance that I could prove to her that I had not had too much to drink, she packaged up the chunk of hair and mailed it to her dad. We had forgotten about sending the hair, not that I'll ever forget those animals, when her dad called a couple of months later. He said he had his lab try to identify it, and they even sent it to a major university, but it came back as "non-identifiable – unknown species." They told Angie's father that it definitely was animal hair, but nothing they had ever seen. He said that everyone in the office that heard the story was extremely curious, and three individuals came up to him throughout the day asking about if he thought it might have been Bigfoot. When he called Angie, they were on the phone quite a while, and when she hung up, she turned to me and said, "Dad asked me if you killed a Bigfoot."

Over the time since that happened, I have talked to a lot of people who live around the area, and several of our neighbors have seen similar of what one man calls "brush apes."

Thad Thomlinson ~ Douglas County, Oregon

A MILE FROM THE BIGFOOT TRAP

Two years ago, my wife and I moved to Medford, Oregon from California; we took an early retirement from our jobs in the aerospace industry. The Sportsman's Warehouse manager overheard our telling his clerk about our scary experience when I was buying a pistol, and he told us about your book, so this is what our first outing produced.

We have always had a desire to do some camping and hiking, so last summer we reserved a space at Hart-Tish Park campground on the Applegate lake. We set out with our new tent trailer, and after setting up camp, we hiked the Collings Mountain trail and visited the "Bigfoot Trap."*

Applegate Lake

64

We had read a few clippings about the Sasquatch, so when we got back to camp we spent a while in the general store inquiring as to whether this animal was real or just something to scare off us "detested Californians." Several people there told us stories about seeing them in the area, and even as sincere as they sounded, we came away feeling that it may be more talk for tourists, because they regaled us with story after story about their customers who had seen the beasts, and we figured they were simply trying to entertain their guests. The next day though, we ended up with our own story!

Remains of a gold miner's cabin near the Bigfoot Trap

We locked up our trailer and drove south to the southern end of the lake and up the dirt road to the Oregon/California border, and then because it just kept climbing, we turned and came back down to the end of the lake, because we wanted to hike rather than drive anymore. We took a dirt road that said "Stein Butte Trailhead;" it went up the opposite side of the lake from our campground. It was called the "Manzanita Creek Road" and we followed it until it crossed Manzanita Creek and started to swing to the left and around and then to the right again up the mountain. Our desire was to do some hiking, but not up in the steep mountains.

We decided to go back to where we had crossed Manzanita Creek and hike along the creek. There was a large area on the left just before we reached the creek, so we parked there, took our small backpacks and headed off on the trail that followed the creek. As we walked, we intersected several trails that went in slightly different directions, and we soon found ourselves on the edge of a beautiful mountain meadow with groves of trees, rocks and just really pretty country. We stuck to the trail that stayed more in the trees as there was so little underbrush. It was such a pleasant outing, and we were enjoying the solitude. Even the few boats and cars seemed to be so far away; we hadn't been in such a quiet environment before and it certainly wasn't like Cali! I didn't mean to ramble, but to us this was like a wilderness adventure!

About a mile or so on this trail we stopped on a sort of flat ledge that ran along and up into the higher elevations, but the trail split soon, and after having a snack and some water, we followed the lesser traveled path downward. We quickly descended and as the trail wrapped to our left, we must have been directly below the upper trail, as a few small rocks came falling down on the path ahead of us. We just assumed that it may have been another hiker, but we didn't see or hear anyone. About another fifty feet ahead it appeared that our trail was about to end, but when we got to some rocks that were blocking it, something jumped up and leaped over the rock barrier and ran noisily down into the deepening gulley on the other side.

We both ran to the large rocks and climbed up so we could see over, and that's when we got a shock that stopped us cold! Expecting to see a deer, I was scrambling in my pack for the camera, but what I was looking at paralyzed me. Not so much in fear, but more in absolute awe. There, moving rapidly along the steep slope of sand and loose rock was a shaggy, brown, long-haired two-legged animal that I couldn't even comprehend!

Then, just as it entered a patch of thick forest that grew at the end of this canyon, another larger animal that looked like a tall gorilla came out of the trees and grabbed the little guy with one hand hoisted it up and onto its shoulder with a giant looking paw, and then almost as in the same motion, threw a large piece of a log in our direction with its other hand! We had to be a hundred feet way, and yet the log sailed right up to where we were standing and we had to jump back to avoid being hit. Naturally, my lack of any outdoor experience caused me to push Carol out of the way and then I fell flat on my face in the rocks, causing enormous embarrassment and numerous cuts and bruises. Carol and I helped each other up, and we looked at each other as if to say, "Did that actually happen?"

Even though these creatures were more afraid of us than even seemed logical with our size differences and our obvious shortcomings in being able to even walk in this terrain, we assumed that they were still moving up the canyon, and sensibly, we decided to retreat and hobble our way back out. We retraced our route, while glancing to our back trail every few minutes until we reached the car and were able to quickly return to our campsite to wash and doctor our wounds.

After cleaning up, and changing out of our torn and soiled clothes, we visited the general store again; only a little more humble and confident that they had two more believers in the Bigfoot creature. We gave them a new story to add to their collection. Although we drew quite an audience of fellow campers and got our experience noted in their "storybook," we had the pride of becoming true Oregonians!

Jim and Carol Longacre ~ Medford, Oregon

The Bigfoot Trap

* Publisher's note: Rumors of Bigfoot sightings came so often in this area that when a group of wildlife researchers from Eugene, Oregon went in search of the mysterious creature; they chose a site on Grouse Creek to build a trap to prove their theories and catch the beast that had everyone so fearful! In the early 1970's, this group constructed a solid wooden structure with heavy steel bars that seems it could hold a huge beast of a gorilla's size and weight. It was built upward from the Collings Trail on a spur not far off the main trail, and about 200 yards away. It was there that it sat for many years without any success except that it was rumored to have captured a hapless deer hunter for a time until he was eventually rescued. Finally, the state ordered the trap permanently disabled so as to protect the public and other wildlife from harm.

FOLLOWING BIGFOOT'S TRAIL

Last fall, I was deer hunting in the coast range up by Tillamook, Oregon with my dad and brother, as we do whenever we get the chance to get off work at the same time; which is about every three years, and I can finally say that I too saw Bigfoot!

Northern Coast Range ~ By M.O. Stevens (Own work) [GFDL (http://www.gnu.org/copyleft/fdl.html) or CC BY-SA 3.0 (http://creativecommons.org/licenses/by-sa/3.0)], via Wikimedia Commons

Our hunt was scheduled for the first three days of the season plus travel time, so we made the trip over from Hillsboro and got our camp set up the night before. Early the next morning we tossed a coin to see who got point, and since I won, I went off to a knoll where we had placed a tree platform, and climbed quietly up and settled into position while Dad and my brother Dan started off to make our usual long, circular drive that has been successful for four out of the last five years.

I was quite well camouflaged and my elevated viewpoint allowed me to see over a far reaching area which was largely covered with tall pines interspersed with blackberry and other patches of brush that could hide a herd of elk; where at eye level, a hunter would never see them. With deer being so much smaller, the tree stand is the only practical way to hunt this area.

After about two hours of slowly trying to watch the area by slightly moving my head and taking care not to make any major moves, I finally saw movement about two hundred feet away from my stand. A sapling moved, and something was pulling it over; I couldn't make out what it was, as I could just see a brown shape in what looked like a fur coat and dark brown hat and gloves bending it slowly down. Then suddenly, whatever it was let go of the tree and it sprang back up, but I noticed that there was a bare spot where it had stripped off the bark about 10 feet up and maybe six inches wide. As I watched this being; I could see now as it continued over a slight rise that this wasn't a human at all, but it was very tall and gorilla-like. It was hard to see anything but part of its head and its arms when it reached up to bend down the tree. Although it looked like an ape, it walked with body motion similar to a man; no slouching, lurching, sideways movement like gorillas, and it was quite thin.

As it made its way farther off to my right, it stopped when it was about two hundred feet down from the first place I saw it, and it bent down another tall sapling and went through the same procedure again. I slowly followed it through my seven power monocular, and wished I had something more powerful, but in this brushy country, optics aren't much good, because you can't see far ahead anyway, and unless you're in a tree, you can't see more than 50 feet.

As I steadied my monocular against my knee, I could see that the animal had again peeled a wide strip of bark off the other tree and let it spring back up. Then this gorilla-like animal turned and walked directly to the right again, and now it was at a right angle to me and heading downhill into the valley below. I wished I had a radio, but Dad would have beaten me silly if I had got on one anyway, because any verbal communicating on our hunts was forbidden.

I sat for another half hour without even a bird coming by when all of a sudden another one of these apelike creatures came into view at the same place I saw the first one, and then straining to see, I thought that it had a smaller one with it! I could just make out its presence when its hairy hand pushed a bush out of its way. The two of them turned again at the tree marked by the first animal, and then I watched as the two of them appeared to be following the first one's trail. I could see part of the bigger one and a glimpse of the small one's hand and head every now and then.

I kept watching as these two Bigfoot stayed on the path of the first one, and precisely at that second tree, the bigger one pointed up to the marking and they both turned and followed the same path downward that the first one made.

Anyway, that's all I can report. My dad, brother and I got together when they unsuccessfully came empty handed to my stand, pushing only themselves and no deer; I told them my story and walked them across to the first sapling, and then to the next, so they could witness the places the big guy had peeled off the bark. It took all three of us to bend it down and examine the peeled areas where Bigfoot did it with one hand!

By this time the sun was racing toward the ocean, and it would soon get dark in these woods, so we removed my tree stand and headed back to camp.

Tillamook Bay ~ CC0 Public Domain (Maxpixel)

While we were cooking dogs on our gas grille, another party of hunters, who were on their way to Tillamook, stopped at our camp to chat. They lived nearby and were just doing day trips, but I excitedly retold my story! I was just so eager to be believed, as Dad and Dan hadn't given me much assurance that they were buying my story. Before I even finished, two of the men were nodding their heads, and when I got to the part of the trail marking, they in unison asked, "About ten feet up and peeled off the bark?" When I asked how they knew, they said they had both seen these trails many times and it was assumed that these Sasquatch, as they called them, were strangers to this particular area, and it was a common practice that the one in charge stayed far ahead for safety of the group, and if it was safe to stop, the leader waited for the others to catch up.

In our years of hunting deer, we had never hunted blacktail, as they are a lot smaller than whitetail or mulies, so this was new to us. It was also shocking for us to find that these hunters who lived here could be so casual and nonchalant about seeing the creature that everyone wonders whether it is even real. Believe you me; Bigfoot is real!

Tommy Thompson Jr. ~ Hillsboro, Oregon

BIGFOOT'S HIDEOUT

My husband I just moved to Rogue River City, Oregon and wanted to explore the beautiful area before we get too old. Ken always wanted a 4-wheel drive so we could have adventure; we went right down a got a new 4x4 pickup and we started to explore our new home.

Ken is in his late 70's and said he wanted to explore while he still can, so we are indulging his wishes and we are both really having fun.

After repeatedly trying to find a road that would take us across the Rogue River to the Almeda Mine* site, we bought your book Hiking Sasquatch Country, because the book store said it was the only way to find it. We read about how many times it took you to find it, so you made it easy for us!

We left home early one morning, as we saw that it meant walking downhill for miles from where you have to park and we wanted to allow lots of time for the more difficult return trip. We parked up above the BLM gate, and we each carried a backpack and extra water. The nice thing about Oregon is that it never seems to get too hot, especially in these pine covered mountains.

Almeda Mine shaft

If you had not described it so well, we may have given up earlier because it seemed like forever before we suddenly came to the middle mine shaft entrance. Too bad it was closed with those iron gates, but the place is super interesting.

We wound down all the way to the bottom entrance and we hiked out to the edge of the Rogue River and then chatted for some time with rafters who had pulled over to rest. They were from Des Moines, Iowa, and I think they'll be moving to Oregon in a couple of years also.

Then, following your guide, we went along the shore a ways and cut up to the shelf where there was evidence of the living quarters you described, and then we went to look at the pieces of equipment, and that's where we saw it!

Rafting on the Rogue River

A big, long-haired, hunched-over animal that resembled a gorilla, but it stood straighter. It had short legs and longer than normal length arms, and I'd say it stood seven to eight feet tall.

For some reason, we were not afraid, and it didn't seem alarmed either. We just stood on that flat ledge; it was slightly above us on the dirt road to the top, and it cocked its head then made a woofing sound, but not very loud. Then, it walked on up the trail while watching us, and then it stopped again and tilted its head, probably wondering if we were real, since neither of us had moved a hair since we saw it. Then Ken tried to communicate with it; he quietly said, "Hello." The second the big fellow heard Ken speak, he bolted off the road and ran up the steep slope above the road. It must have gone two hundred feet and never once looked back, and within a minute or so it had disappeared.

Ken's been kicking himself ever since, but who would ever guess? Hindsight of course it great, but we wondered if possibly we could have moved enough without disturbing it to get the camera, but anyway it was really quite a thrill!

Abandoned piece of equipment at the Almeda Mine

Discussing our adventure afterward, as we had the three hours of hill to climb on the road back, I had a fleeting first thought that it might have been a hoax for tourists, but Ken reminded me that it was so hard to get here, and as your book said, it was also posted "no trespassing," but we never saw the signs.

All in all, this was probably the most exciting thing that we've ever experienced in our travels, and hope you can use it in one of the true stories of encounters, because believe me, we had one!

Helen Rohrbaugh ~ Rogue River, Oregon

Looking down at the Rogue River from the Almeda Mine

* *Publisher's note: The road is posted "no trespassing" due to the fact that before Oregon legalized marijuana, this area had several illegal pot growers camping out near several mountain streams and growing their crops in these massive forests. It is quite safe to travel through here as long as one does not go too far off the main road.*

OREGON CAVES SASQUATCH

My wife Pat and I had often traveled to Oregon on our summer vacations as we are both in the teaching profession, so we make it a point to set aside an entire month each year to travel and sightsee, but with an ulterior motive. We are looking for the ideal climate for retirement and we do know that Montana is great for earning a living, but we will be saying adios in five more years and Oregon seems to be our choice.

I wanted to submit our story for your latest book if it's not too late. Please use the alias we show, as on this particular trip we used a little white lie as to why we missed a teacher's conference the year of this adventure; we told them we were out of the country and couldn't return on time, and since the conference had not been scheduled before we left, we got away with it.

We stayed in southern Oregon for three weeks and drove down to Crescent City, California and then as far north as Newport, Oregon and generally scouted out the area for our future move after our retirements.

On our way back south, we stayed in Cave Junction, Oregon and took two days to explore the area around the Oregon Caves National Monument. That's where we had the scariest time of our lives! I will however have to admit that it was an adventure we would not trade, because it was truly the most excitement we ever have had, before or since. Even though it was a frightening experience, it was wonderful!

We had toured the cave and had a reservation that evening right there in the Chateau, and we had a very enjoyable time eating, hanging out, and visiting with the chateau personnel and visitors.

Chateau at the Oregon Caves

We met some folks from California that told us about the hike they had taken that morning and they said they had seen what the on-duty park ranger told them was a Bigfoot! We had dinner with these people that night and they had a really interesting story about their morning hike. They described a rather easy and pleasant trek, and told us about stepping off the trail at a place where they could hear sounds like a waterfall, so they followed the sound to hopefully take some scenic photos when they came face to face with what they described as a large, shaggy creature that they immediately assessed to be a Sasquatch!

They were from northern California, and were quite aware of many Bigfoot sightings in their mountains and throughout Oregon, although it was the first one they had ever seen. The ranger they reported the sighting to, had asked them to keep quiet about their experience so as not to frighten the tourists, so they were telling us this in hushed tones that added to our excitement.

The next morning we looked over our collection of trail maps and determined that we would follow the same trail that these people had told us about the previous evening, but knowing full well that the animal was not likely to be posing for photos, we were still hoping to maybe photograph a footprint or something to tell the grandkids about.

Pathway after exiting the Oregon Caves

The trail the people had told us about dropped downhill from the Chateau, but when we started down where they told us, there was a big "trail maintenance" sign placed directly over the path with another sign stapled on it that said "do not enter."

Evidently the rangers didn't want anyone else seeing the wild Bigfoot, so we dug into our map bag and saw another trail that led further west from the Chateau, but it went a long way down the mountain and then it showed it coming back up again and crossed Cave Creek to the same area that these other folks had told us where they had their sighting and it was named *No Name Trail*, and it followed *No Name Creek* down the mountain.

No Name Trail ~ By the National Park Service

We had the entire day ahead of us, so we figured, "Why not?" We would come up from the other direction and since the easy trail was blocked, we'd work a little harder to get there, but the odds were that we'd probably be the only people on the trail, because we were told by many people that for the most part, tourists visited the main sights and attractions, while only the residents had the time for the hikes. It was a beautiful day although fairly cool at this high altitude, but we had dressed warmly.

Cliff Nature Trail ~ By the National Park Service

We traveled well past the chateau and the *Cliff Nature Trail* and started downward on our journey past the end of the long parking lot area where our trail headed kind of northwest according to my cellphone compass, but it kept jumping around, so we guessed the mountain must have iron in it, but the path was clear.

As steep as this route was, we were a bit concerned about the return trip back up, but we kept going and dropping steadily downward. We were about halfway around as near as we could tell and there was a sign that indicated No Name Creek cutting off to our left, so we made the short detour and the scenery that we passed through was breathtaking!

After having a snack and resting a bit, we went back from No Name Creek and picked up the main trail again and followed it as it curved back up to our right until we came to a junction that showed Cave Creek Campground to the left and the Caves Chateau to the right, so we kept to the right. Just then we crossed Cave Creek and there was a large sign and a well-used trail. We had not gone even a hundred feet when we heard a loud noise to our right and it sounded like something splashing in the water, so we very carefully and stealthily as city people can be, made our way to the source of the sounds. We came to a spot where three enormous pine trees were growing so close together there was no underbrush around them. Crouching and moving slowly, we moved in between the giants and we both peered around opposite sides of the same tree, and I guess the fitting term would be, we were both flabbergasted!

There in a fairly deep pool under a small, wide waterfall about three feet high were two beings that could have been human children, but they were covered all over with light brown to tan hair, and it's so hard to even describe them from such a short encounter, because as we moved back behind the tree to make certain we were both seeing the same thing, a loud thud echoed from the forest; it sounded like a deep thump of a rock or something heavy hitting against a tree, and it was followed by three raps like a stick against another stick. As we quickly turned our attention back to the pool, the two hairy ones were on their way up the hill on all fours, and in a few seconds not even a tree branch moved.

Later as we compared notes, we both concur that these animals seemed to have been playing in the water, much like human children. We concluded that they had to be the Sasquatch, but they did not move or run like small apes as other people have reported. They didn't lurch from side to side like chimpanzees and they didn't have long monkey arms, nor did they make the rocking back and forth motions like apes do. They seemed to have human-like legs and bodies; with maybe slightly longer arms. Their faces were brown and kind of shiny, with very little hair. We also noticed their hands seemed fairly large, and we don't even remember what their ears looked like.

This encounter in such a remote feeling mountain side was not in the least bit frightening, and it is one that neither of us will ever forget! We will very soon be Oregon residents, and we are both looking forward to researching the Sasquatch, as we can honestly tell the world; we saw them!

Paul and Mary Peters ~ Helena, Montana

ON POINT WITH BIGFOOT

Last autumn my dad and I were hunting whitetail deer in western Idaho, as the family, including my grandparents and uncles have always done. I had just served a four year hitch in the Marines and was ready to get into the family business, so this was my welcome home before my break-in to work.

Whitetail buck ~ By werner22brigitte (Pixabay)

Well, being the newcomer, I was placed on point, and the first drive of the day would begin as soon as I made my way to the head of the low pass, the others would circle the large wooded hills whose runoff fed the creek that ran nearby. It took them awhile to drive their trucks in opposite directions, so I prepared for a long wait. I settled in at a comfortable and well-concealed spot where I overlooked a wide, long valley.

As I was sitting whittling on a piece of branch I heard a noise coming from behind me, so I laid my knife and wood down and slowly retrieved my rifle from the tree branch it rested against, and ever so slowly brought it into position across my lap. I just sat there as still as I could, and over my left shoulder I heard something step close to me; thinking it was a deer, I very carefully, using my thumb and forefinger in a pushing and holding maneuver that silently took the safety off my rifle without the slightest perceptible sound or motion. With my finger positioned on the trigger guard so I could quickly fire, I began an ever so slow turning of only my head. When I had turned just a bit, I observed something that made me almost lose control and I credit my sniper training in the Corps that allowed me to not totally lose it!

There, looking directly into my eyes was a monkey-like animal about four to five feet high and covered with orangish-brown hair or fur. We kept staring at each other and it was being as cautious as I was. Like myself, I couldn't see it move anything but its eyes and I tried to carefully turn my shoulders a slight bit more to ease the pain in my neck, and even though its eyes indicated that it saw my movement, it remained still. It had a light brown face that was almost without the hair that covered its head and shoulders, and I tried hard to form a picture that I could remember. Its fingers were like humans, and its hands looked similar to ours, only much longer and wider than human, and I couldn't make out if it had fingernails, but it seemed like it had curved, short claws. Its feet were long and wide and I couldn't see if they had claws, but they seemed furrier. Its eyes were a brownish to reddish color in the sun, and its short ears were covered in longer hair, so I don't know what they looked like.

We must have stayed like that for at least two to three minutes, maybe longer, but I was really in a quandary; I didn't want to shoot it and I didn't want to frighten it, but I wasn't afraid of it. As my mind raced to figure what to do next, I was startled and almost messed my pants by what happened next!

From directly behind me came the most god awful sound I have ever heard. It was a combination of a roar, snarl and screech; the likes of which I had never heard came from right behind me! I sprang to my feet, whirled my gun, safety off, and prepared to protect myself from a monster.

I was facing a large lodgepole pine that was just feet behind me, but no monster! The terrible sound had come from behind the knoll I was on and just downhill from the tree, and as I jumped to the side of the pine, I caught a glimpse of a large arm and the head of a huge gorilla-like form as it disappeared into the deep, thick forest below. I quickly whirled back around and the smaller one was gone. I sprinted to where it had been hoping to see it as it ran down into the dense evergreens below, but it was long gone.

When Dad and the other drivers finally came from both directions, all they were pushing in front of them were three chipmunks and four blue jays. Although disappointed, I burst out with my story, and to my surprise, they all smiled and laughed knowingly. They told me that they had heard the shriek from the monster, and then while we were returning to our rigs, they regaled me with incidents surrounding what they said were Sasquatch.

Evidently a family of them had moved into these mountains about three years before, and although they were not causing any problems, other than the occasional stolen chicken, rabbit or lamb. When they were close like today, the deer avoided being anywhere near. The next morning we went to the other side of the mountain and filled our tags in two days.

I did want to submit this story because our Fish and Game officer told us about your books; hope you can use it.

Brad Hendershot ~ Coeur d'Alene, Idaho

BIGFOOT ON THE ROGUE RIVER

We were hiking along the Rogue River last winter along the shore near Hellgate canyon, as this is about the only time of year when you can genuinely enjoy the beautiful Rogue without standing in line behind tourists.

Looking toward the Hellgate Bridge on the Rogue River

Seldom do we get a chance to get photos of animals with rafts floating by at 10 minute intervals and the jet boats playing at making giant waves, so we took our Shepherd out for a long romp along the river. We had hiked up river from the parking area below Hellgate and it was threatening to rain, but a perfect day for the ducks and geese that were all over the place.

Hellgate Canyon Viewpoint ~ By Greg Shine, BLM

We were watching to see what had stirred up a large murder* of crows way upon the other side of the river. They seemed to be going absolutely nuts, so I got the camera out of my backpack while my wife managed our dog, Wolf. The sun was fighting to get through the clouds and I was straining to get my focus on the spot way up the steep mountain across the river, just to be ready for a lucky photo op of a bear or coyote, since it normally takes some bigger event to get crows that excited; they must have been anticipating a kill of some magnitude and lots of leftover meat scraps.

There must have been over 30 crows and they were really making a racket, when all of a sudden, a man ran out into the gap in the trees, and on his shoulder was a small deer. Then, as I triggered the shot, I saw what I had assumed to be a man was actually a stooped-over being that resembled a large chimpanzee, so I snapped two more shots before it disappeared into the pines again.

Paula had been watching the scene, and she actually saw it better, because I was busy trying to see it on my Cannon's small screen, which was like looking into a lightbulb for all the good it was, and so I had pointed and shot. The results; not a chance! Just a nice sun's reflection with a few pine trees and rocks.

Paula did get a chance to view the animal, and her only statement was an excited, "That was a Bigfoot! We really saw a Bigfoot!" Well, she did, and I only saw the sun. Paula said that it was hard to guess its size as the distance was probably two football fields away and up at about 45 degrees, but she it guessed it must have been bigger than me, as she compared it against an old fence line on the mountain side across from us which would have made the animal well over six or seven feet tall and she noted it was very wide through the shoulders. She said she'd have hated to see me tangle with it. We own a clothing store in the area, and she said, "We couldn't fit that guy with anything in stock!" We jokingly agreed that I couldn't shoot a Sasquatch with a Canon.

Jack T. ~ Grants Pass, Oregon

* Publisher's note: A group of crows is referred to as a "murder." The website quora.com says, "There are several different explanations for the origin of this term, mostly based on old folk

tales and superstitions: For instance, there is a folktale that crows will gather and decide the capital fate of another crow. Many view the appearance of crows as an omen of death because ravens and crows are scavengers and are generally associated with dead bodies, battlefields, and cemeteries and they're thought to circle in large numbers above sites where animals or people are expected to soon die. But the term 'murder of crows' mostly reflects a time when groupings of many animals had colorful and poetic names."

By falco (Pixabay)

BITTEN BY SASQUATCH

A rafting trip down the "Wild and Scenic" Rogue River in Southern Oregon was a dream vacation that my roommate Peter and I had often fantasized about while pursuing our rapidly progressing careers in information technology. Alas, we determined that such things were made to hang out there to dream about while focusing on the ultimate goal; success in business.

After post graduate work was completed, we had planned to make our trip as a reward for finally reaching our first objective. Peter had secured a great spot in a San Francisco top 500 company and I had succeeded in capturing a prize position out of a field of over 400 applicants, and in three weeks I was reporting to Intel in Hillsboro, Oregon.

We had already paid our deposits with a reputable rafting company, and a week before our departure, Peter came down with appendicitis. There went our trip and our deposit, and by the time Peter was ready to head to Cali, I was being fitted at Nordstrom, so as to make a good first impression in what I anticipated would secure my future.

Peter and I stayed in touch throughout the next 15 years, but careers being what they are, we now were involved with local friendships. We did get together on a few occasions, but never for too long at a time. Then as things sometimes happen, I had received notice from my employer about a pending merger or corporate restructuring, and I was facing a three week layoff with pay. As I contemplated my options for the future and began wondering what to do for a few weeks in the interim, the phone rang and it was Peter!

He was in Oregon on a month's leave of absence because his father had just passed away, and he had not had time to do anything but pack a bag and barely made it to the hospital in Eugene. When he entered his dad's room, he said his father opened his eyes and asked, "What took you so long?" Those were his last words. I silently shed tears with Peter, and he said he was crushed even though he and his father were not close; they were so alike that Peter needed to get away. We both looked at each other and realized this was our chance! The next day Peter had bid goodbye to his few remaining relatives as all arrangements had been made, and he told everyone he just needed to spend some time in solitude.

Our trip was on! Naturally every available rafting company was booked solid, but one friendly owner suggested that we check with the Rand ranger station on the Rogue River for any private cancellations, because private parties have to have reservations the same as the rafting companies do. Our first call was a success! A party of three had just cancelled a few hours before and we jumped on it. Now we had a real dilemma; we could easily afford to purchase a raft and every kind of equipment we would need, but we had to somehow get trained in how to raft a large and dangerous river. The Rogue River is a killer; it's not like simply floating gently down the stream. There is a long, long list of victims claimed by the Rogue!

Acting on a chance, I called the raft rental owner back who had given us the lead on the ranger station and profusely thanked him, and then I explained our situation and asked him if we came down to Grants Pass the next day if he could completely outfit us for the trip with everything from paddles to coolers, and most importantly, if he could find a licensed guide who we could hire as our pilot. Minutes later the man called me back and we were on. I gave him my credit card number and told him to "treat me fair," but get it booked as we had only four days until our permits were active.

The next day, we two old friends were at long last ready to fulfill a 20 year old dream. I am giving you this with as much detail as I can, as it is indelibly imprinted into my memory, and it was truly an amazing set of coincidences that were more like a dream than reality.

Small rapids on the Rogue River near the Grave Creek boat launch

A few days later, the dream now became a reality which morphed into a combination of a haunting and fearsome recurring dream. The vision has remained etched in my senses even after all this time. Maybe sharing the experience will help, so I'm submitting this story to hopefully make it into your next book. When I told Peter, he was thrilled with the idea of sharing our adventure, even though it was horrible at times.

We left at dawn on a Thursday from the Grave Creek boat launch, as we could leave our car fairly secure and take a shuttle back from Gold Beach once we hit the take out at the Rogue's mouth. Our guide, Walt, was a retired gentleman of some years who said he had been close friends with many of the famous pioneer rafters such as Glen Wooldridge, whose book "The Rogue: A River To Run" I have a copy of.

Rafters on the Rogue River

After our second day, we were all taking turns steering the raft, cooking, setting up camp and clean up. The weather was beautiful, although the sun was scorching on our right side, so we tried to keep to the left of the river when we could, but the Rogue is vicious and demanded its own way!

There were rafters ahead and behind, and I recall them saying that a new party was released every 10 minutes. Toward late afternoon, many parties had pulled over already to enjoy camp-life and stretch out the kinks when we began searching in earnest for a spot away from any groups not knowing what kind of neighbors they would be and to enjoy some much needed solitude.

Our guide was an absolute gem; not too talkative until brought into the conversation, but once he began he went on for hours with a dissertation about life on the river that held us both spellbound. Peter and I both freely admit that this was a once in a lifetime experience that likely will rank as the most enjoyable times that either of us ever in our lives had spent; or probably ever will! Even after the upcoming event that marked a gruesome turn, we came away with a new appreciation of life!

The next morning we leisurely awaited the passing of a large, joyous flotilla of merrymakers that all seemed to be shouting at the same time; there were about 15 rafts within yards of each other and it looked as if a county fair had fallen off into the river and the fairgoers had not yet noticed as they continued their revelry.

We entered the river after things were back to nature again, and around the next bend, which I believe was close to an old

Chinese mining claim according to my map, there was a sort of marshy inlet off to the side. We agreed to go closer so we could view a pair of beautiful blue herons that seemed to be feasting in the shallow pool. The birds however, were not the least bit interested in making new friends and they left us a few squawks in protest as they launched up and over the grasses to the quiet waters further on.

We decided to enter this shallow lagoon on the off chance that its bottom might somehow be laden with that spectacle of gold miners dreams that would reveal a bowl glinting of gold washed down from the Chinese mines and secured for a century by this hidden cove. Since we all three had this same visual image as we shared our thoughts aloud; we had little choice but to step out of our raft and pull it over the lagoon's rim; reentering it once we were again afloat. Alas; even stirring at the bottom with our paddles yielded nothing but weeds and long rotting muck. After enjoying the solitude of our secret cove and watching several jubilant rafters passing by with no knowledge of our presence, we decided it was time to get back to our trek.

We paddled to a spot that looked like an easier barrier to overcome, and as the raft settled on the river's edge again, we saw what appeared to be the body of a large, furry animal just inside the breakwater, so we slowly paddled closer. At first we thought the animal was a large bear, although it was a light brown color rather than the black and brown of the local bears, and it was also huge. Laboring a while to reach it because of having to fight the paddles as they were being enveloped by the dense marsh grass, we carefully paddled to where we could reach out a grab hold of the hairy beast. There we finally were; all three of us on the same side of the raft, and it took everything we had to barely turn the animal to view it more carefully. That's where the shock hit us all right smack into an almost fearful apprehension that something didn't fit!

This was not a bear, and not anything any of us had ever before seen in our lives! It was a tall, extremely hairy and very heavy creature with seemingly long legs, very long arms, and very long fingers, but no claws. It took a major effort to bring its face into view, and when we could splash enough water over it to clean off the muck, we found the face to be almost gone. Some critters; turtles, birds or others had evidently been feeding on this carcass, as the eyes, nose, cheeks, jowls and throat had all been eaten away, and pushing a knife into these areas disturbed many hundreds of whitish, worm-like maggots or whatever; we quickly tired of our autopsy. The ears were also chewed somewhat, but they were small and almost not there, except for the inner ear, where again those damned gross worms were packed thickly inside.

The animal was now more bottom heavy, and it may have been that we had disturbed the body so that its feet were now floating, whereas before, they may have been anchoring it to the bottom somehow. We struggled to slip a rope around its arms and barely made one loop under its heavy left arm when a wave from a swollen rapid hit it front on, spinning it wildly as the three of us made a superhuman effort to get a loop around the other arm, and we also managed to get two quick loops around its neck. Until now, comparing notes afterward, Peter and I were still under the assumption that we were trying to retrieve a dead bear, and without any more motive than the thrill of discovery and adding to our adventure.

Class IV Tyee Rapids on the Rogue River

Suddenly in a loud, gruff announcement, with our catch fairly secured to our raft, Walt, our guide, triumphantly balanced as best he could with an oar, and bracing himself against the bumper on the raft; he announced, "Gentlemen, we have captured a Bigfoot!" As if reading our bewildered expressions, he repeated in a loud, crowing voice, "You know; a Sasquatch! This is going to put us front page on every newspaper in America!" He continued his excited tirade saying we would all be famous.

Just at that exact moment, our raft edged out into the rapids of the Rogue and we were assaulted by a huge, pounding blast from a wave that cascaded over a monstrous boulder; it hit us broadside and stood our raft on its side, and only by the grace of God were we not capsized! Everything that wasn't tightly tied down was totally gone into the river.

Standing on end for a split second, our raft suddenly and violently flapped down on the water with a deafening crash, and the three of us, still holding on to the myriad of ropes with fingers, toes and legs wrapping into anything that could stabilize us, were suddenly on our backs in the cold water. Sadly, our Bigfoot had been reclaimed by the Rogue!

I believe that the frightening realization that we were all alive after a crash in one of the most highly dangerous sections of this entire river, and only due to the last second flip of the raft where it could have just as easily gone over with us entangled upside down, we all likely would have drowned without a chance! We were all exhausted to the max, but we knew there was still grave danger, as we were careening through a terrifying area at a rapid pace without having any control!

I never have been able to figure out how I or the others had become so wrapped up in the ropes, and in reminiscing; the only thing that makes sense is that it was an automatic reaction by the human mind of basic survival; anything to clutch at and everything that gave any ray of hope! Fortunately, the spare paddle was still lashed to the inside of the raft, and Walt immediately and automatically unlashed it and took control; issuing orders for Peter and me as to how to assist him with our raft again plunging back into the frightening maelstrom.

We quickly checked for leaks and holes, secured our remaining equipment and scanned the river for our lost supplies. Downstream a few yards, floated our large chest that housed food and water, and Walt soon managed to maneuver us to recapture it, so now we were certain of survival!

Being thoroughly exhausted and thankful to be alive, we sought out the nearest suitable spot to pull over, and when the raft was secure, we pulled our remaining equipment, cooler and paddles out, laid them on the sand and simultaneously we collapsed in unison on the warm sand; promptly falling asleep. About an hour later we stirred and gradually began putting our lives back together.

For the rest of the evening, Walt regaled us with stories of the mysterious Bigfoot animals, that up until now, we had been blissfully ignorant of. The existence of the animals had never even entered into any conversation or news that Peter or I had ever been party to. Walt had an encyclopedic sort of knowledge of these beings, and as we listened, we became enthralled with the discovery of such an animal existing among us. We both admittedly were amazed that there could be so much history and information of a species living among us that until we held its body in our arms, we were completely unaware of.

Comparing notes for hours, we believe this Bigfoot to have been around seven feet tall, with shorter legs in proportion to its long torso, much longer arms with long fingers, and its feet were wide with short, fat toes. It had body hair everywhere except over its ruggedly weathered face, at least what was left of it, and the rest of our brief experience has pretty much become a blur.

When we finally drifted to a passing sheriff's river patrol, they assisted us by helping get us off the river and escorted us back to the Assante Three Rivers Medical Center in Grants Pass. We all had multiple cuts, bruises, scrapes and lumps. Walt had a fractured collar bone, but not serious enough to hold the tough old bird down. What a great friend and what a fine man he turned out to be! I had a deep gouge on my palm and a large cut across my forearm which I remembered had happened when I ended up struggling to secure the Sasquatch creature and caught myself in his mouth when the raft spun up, so I was given a series of painful injections.

I feel qualified to go on record as having been bitten by Bigfoot; too bad I didn't even get a tooth! Thanks for the listen.

Brendan Winslow II ~ Lake Oswego, Oregon

RAINIE FALLS SASQUATCH

My sister Sandy and I had a very scary encounter on the Rogue River when we visited in Glendale, Oregon in 2008. We never told anyone but a few friends, because we returned to our home in Redding, California shortly afterward. A story like this must be reserved only for a very close group of friends so you won't be construed to be a "nut case!"

Sandy and I had both been attending the U of O in Eugene, Oregon, and our parents were living in Redding, but were looking at purchasing a home with a few acres of land near Glendale; we coordinated our trip home after our last semester to meet our parents and an Oregon Realtor at their hopefully, new home. We had booked rooms in the town of Grants Pass, as the pickings for accommodations in Glendale were doubtful at best.

We all liked the property the folks had picked out, so after discussing it over dinner, Mom and Dad decided to make an offer and enter into serious negotiations the next morning. So Sis and I decided to hang around Grants Pass and after taking a jet boat trip the next day on the wild Rogue River, where we went all the way through Hellgate Canyon, we both had a desire to see more of this magnificent and wild river from the shore so we could take some photos.

The following day the folks put the final agreement together and signed papers that made them "Oregonians," so Sandy and I planned our day hiking venture.

Grave Creek flowing into the Rogue River

Early the next morning we arrived at the Grave Creek boat landing, but the long, steep drive down the hill to the parking area was an absolute traffic jam. There must have been a dozen vehicles jockeying for the boat launch and all of the parking spots looked like they were full, so vehicles were launching their rafts and then driving back up the steep hill to park their rigs along the narrow, paved road across the bridge on both sides. Fortunately for us, I had not yet entered the downward road, so with a few waves and "thank yous," I backed out of the line and drove back across the bridge and parked half on the shoulder and half in the shallow ditch; there were vehicles up and down the road parked the same way.

The Rogue River near the beginning of the Rainie Falls Hiking Trail

As we were heading on foot for the long trip over the bridge and walking through the traffic jam some hikers on the near side of the river were returning to their car and exclaimed to us how much they had enjoyed their hike. We told them that we thought that the south trail dead-ended really close in, but they said it went all the way past Rainie Falls, and was really pretty with less foot traffic than the other side of the river, so we happily changed our minds. The trail on the north side of the Rogue River goes all the way to the Pacific Ocean, but the south side is inaccessible for the most part.

This truly was a beautiful hike. It had rained hard the previous evening and the trail was quite slippery and with few footprints. We were glad to have our aluminum hiking sticks, because at times, walking along the very narrow and slippery trail alongside a hundred foot cliff mere inches from your outside foot gives one an eerie feeling.

View of the Rogue River and Sanderson Island from the Rainie Falls Hiking Trail

We did meet another older couple who were locals; they told us the falls were named after J. N. Rainie* who had a cabin nearby and made a living netting salmon and selling them to the area's inhabitants who were mainly gold miners; he made deliveries as far away as Glendale, Oregon. Mr. Rainie was found robbed and murdered in his cabin in the late 1920's.

We took our time and had a beautiful hike until we finally ran out of trail at the falls. We sat down to munch on some granola and treat ourselves to a few sips water as we enjoyed watching the falls; we even caught sight of a few fish jumping.

Rather than just turn back, I wanted to push the issue, so I convinced Sandy to continue our hike down the Rogue on this very tiny ledge where we finally ended up clutching the sides of the steep overhanging rock ledges, and using toe holds, we made a few more feet of progress.

We had descended really close to the water by now and finally we had nowhere left to move. The Rogue River is very swift and unforgiving, as people had told us, and if we fell in, the rapids would have grabbed us and ended any chance of survival even though we are both excellent swimmers.

Rainie Falls

So there we were; attached to the sheer rock face by only toes and fingernails when suddenly a small rockslide came rumbling down from the steep hill between our sanctuary and the huge boulder fifteen feet downriver!

We both looked up over the short rock wall we were clinging to and on the steep, pine covered cliff side high above there were rocks and dirt cascading down a deep "V" shaped gully and plummeting down to the river's edge.

We saw the source of the rockslide at the exact same time, because I heard Sandy's audible gasp as I forced out a "Look!" Then we both just stared dumbfounded and speechless.

There, making a hasty retreat into a growth of pines was a creature on two legs, covered with a dark brown to black coat of hair, with long arms stretching out to the spindly saplings ahead to quickly pull itself into a dense thicket of pines. Then, except for two separate and short rockslides, all was again silent and the river reclaimed all sounds.

We quickly made the wise move to edge our way back to the trail, as our fingers and toes were about ready to abandon us to the river below if we persisted in pushing them any longer. We made our way quickly to very solid ground and collapsed against a low rock to compare notes; the realization set in that Sasquatch really does exist!

We will swear to it forever, because we both were discussing our experience with friends on many occasions since that adventure and we have at times, as a test, sat in separate areas and made our notes and comments in minute detail and our observations are exactly the same.

We have both since graduated and gone our separate ways, but whenever we gather with family and friends, we enjoy reminiscing about our most exciting adventure ever in a lifetime!

We always talk about making a return trip to Rainie Falls, and we hope to find the time to do it in the near future, although next time, we'll make the falls our turnaround point.

Marty A. ~ Salem, Oregon

* *Publisher's note: Rainie Falls was named for Mr. J.N. Rainie who lived in a cabin at the foot of the rapids. He worked a placer claim when he first arrived on the river and later he earned a steady income for himself by gaffing salmon at the falls and selling them in the town of Glendale. J.N. Rainie was found dead in his cabin in the late 1920's, and like so many murders that happened along the Rogue River, it was never solved. The Rogue River was known for the disappearances of large numbers of people!*

STATE OF JEFFERSON BIGFOOT

I live in Yreka, California with my husband and 12 year-old daughter. My husband works for a construction company and sometimes has to spend a week or two away from home. This June while he was away, I decided to take a road trip with my daughter Abigail and visit some friends who live in southern Oregon.

We followed I-5 north to Ashland and spent a week with one of my college pals. From there we went to Grants Pass to take one of the Hellgate boat trips and explore the antique stores on Sixth Street. The next morning we followed the Redwood Hwy. to Cave Junction to spend another week with my oldest and dearest friend Betty.

When it was time to return home, I decided to take the back roads through Happy Camp and on to Yreka; it takes an hour or so longer, but it's a lovely drive. I knew my husband wouldn't like us traveling the lonely distance by ourselves, so I didn't tell him when I called to let him know we were getting ready to go home.

After a leisurely breakfast, we said our goodbyes to Betty and her family and took Rockydale to Waldo Road and it soon turned into Happy Camp Road. It's a bit confusing here because the Happy Camp Road is also called Grayback Road and Indian Creek Road.

I guess I drank too much coffee that morning, because after only 30 minutes, I desperately needed a potty-break. Thank goodness the Page Mountain Sno-Park was only a few miles further, where I knew there were vault toilets in the parking area.

I went in to use the facility and told Abigail to stay inside the car with the doors locked. There was no one around and we hadn't passed another vehicle, but you never know what can happen in these wild mountains. When I came back out, she had gotten out of the car and was reading the sign board that tells about the State of Jefferson*.

As I was standing there scolding her, we heard something that sounded like pounding out in the nearby woods. At first it sounded very near the parking lot, and then there was the sound of more pounding from farther away. We turned to see what was making the noise, and there was a very large animal standing on its hind legs. It had a piece of dead tree in one of its front paws and was getting ready to hit it against the enormous pine it was standing near.

Abigail yelled "Bear" and we both ran to the car and jumped in! From the relative safety of the car we continued to watch the bear, but it wasn't a bear. The animal was standing straight, not hunched over at all. Its fur was sort of a cinnamon color and was much longer than a bear's coat. Its face didn't seem to have much hair on it, nor did its hands. Abigail and I shouted at the same second; "That's a Bigfoot!"

We were too far away from it to make eye contact and we didn't feel it was threatening us in any manner, but we didn't want to take any chances and wanted to be on our way.

When we arrived home my husband Steve was there and I had to come clean about the route we came home by. He stood there and looked at me for a few minutes and told me not to ever do that again. Abigail and I recounted our story at the dinner table that night, and then Steve and I both encouraged her not to share this story with her friends! She agreed, but who knows what will happen when she returns to school in the fall.

Maxine ~ Yreka, California

*   *Publisher's note: The submitter of this encounter said her daughter had been reading the sign referencing the State of Jefferson, and since visitors to Southern Oregon and Northern California are*

constantly confronted with signs and references to this mythical state, we would like to clear up any mystery, because this entire area came within a day of becoming the 49th state of the United States; Jefferson, USA!

Visitors to southern Oregon often ask about all of the references to the State of Jefferson. You see them everywhere; automobile license frames, shirts, bumper stickers, a radio station, a band, and numerous other suggestions that there is something behind it all.

Occasionally, a reference is made to the "mythical" State of Jefferson. Was it a myth or a story dreamed up by locals to entertain tourists? No, not at all! In fact, had it not been for a cruel twist of fate, you could very well be able to visit Jefferson, USA.

Let's look back on Oregon's early history in order to understand the long road to secession. When this part of the United States was first becoming a focal point for the westward movement, the Mormon and California trails went southward, and the Oregon Trail led down the Columbia River as far as The Dalles. From this point on, the only proven, though exceptionally dangerous, route was by barge downriver to Fort Vancouver, under British control, or Portland and Oregon City on the south side of the mighty waterway.

It took a long time before any land route was explored, and then, only to reach the city of Portland. Once in Portland, one could travel by ship to the Pacific Ocean, and then go south to ports in Southern Oregon and California. The alternative route was to head south of Portland through the fertile Willamette Valley. The dream of most settlers as they traversed the dangerous country to reach Oregon was the prospect of the perfect climate for growing crops throughout the long and wide Willamette Valley.

The expansive Oregon Territory was a hotly contested prize for the country that could lay claim to her. The remoteness kept the importance of such a huge, unexplored territory from the immediate attention, as the United States had little influence in the area, and the British were primarily introduced to the vast holdings by explorers and entrepreneurs with the Hudson's Bay Company. The British were in control of the area as far as it was necessary for a harmonious relationship with their "less civilized" American neighbors.

With the British controlling the entrance to the Columbia River at what is now the Port of Astoria, and with their Fort Vancouver, America began to worry about the very real possibility of the British closing access to shipping, and confiscation of the small American force's weapons! Had this happened, there would have certainly been a seizure of the majority of the as-yet unsettled Oregon Territory from Oregon through what is now the state of Washington, and thus connecting with the already British controlled Canada. America knew it had to act fast in case of this very real possibility of the capture of the Columbia River and Portland, therefore the Applegate Trail was a lifesaver.

The Applegate Trail came about after the Applegate family lost two children in attempting the Columbia route from The Dalles. In 1846, Jesse Applegate and party sought out a new route directly into southern Oregon. This was the perfect solution to America's answer to the British problem. Now, no matter what happened, we had a route with which we could reinforce our area from the south! Soon after, the British withdrew to the Canadian territory, and we were free to lay claim to some of the richest and most beautiful country in America.

When gold was discovered in Oregon soon after the 1848 strikes in California, fortune seekers came from across the country. Ships docking in Portland had the same problems they were having all over California. The crews were jumping ship and heading for the gold fields!

Southern Oregon was soon broiling with thousands of gold seekers. The hills were filled with miners, working wall to wall, along rivers and streams throughout the area, from what is now Interstate Highway 5, all the way to the Pacific Ocean.

One huge strike was "Sailors Diggings," which went through many name changes, with the last and current name being Waldo. When Waldo's gold was almost depleted, the residents dug up the city itself for the riches underneath. The empty land can be observed today as mute testament to the temporary and fleeting life of a gold town.

Thus the future of the area went, as the initial easy pickings played out, and the mining grew into just a steady job without the glamorous strikes. Miners left in large numbers, in search of the glory of new discoveries, always looking for the mother lode!

No attempt had really been made to develop roads throughout this vast area of Southern Oregon and Northern California. The territory that encompasses a geographical area roughly the size of the state of Washington is beautiful, but rugged and untamed. There are areas in these mountains where no human being has ever set foot, and for good reason.

The taxes from the respective states were high for the fact that the residents received no services. Even the state line was not defined, and one could only guess in these mountainous regions. When the California tax collector came to call, the miners swore they were in Oregon, and when the Oregon tax collector came by, they swore to be Californians!

Travel was really dangerous, and even into the late 1930's, those travelling by automobile through this area were advised to carry abundant provisions, along with pick, axe, shovel, and even dynamite to clear the roads which were subject to washouts and landslides. Kind of a "build your own road as you go" plan.

Even though the tax districts were soon straightened out, and the taxes were diligently collected, there were really no benefits to those paying these taxes. All petitions to the respective state governments for passable roads, and the benefits received by the other state residents, went ignored. The people of this huge area felt they were forgotten. Finally, by 1941, after meetings throughout the area from the Cascade Mountains to the Southern Willamette Valley of Oregon, to the Sacramento Valley of California, the populace decided as a whole that the only way to survive was to become their own legally recognized state of the Union. With their own state, their common interests could be of more benefit to themselves and to the United States as well.

The legal secession grew roots, and soon elections were being held throughout the territory. It was decided that the new state would honor President Thomas Jefferson, and Judge John L. Childs of Crescent City, California was elected governor. The Jefferson state capitol was in Yreka. Conflicting versions of the seceding counties sometimes arise, however, the predominant consensus is that the Oregon counties were Coos, Douglas, Curry, Josephine, Jackson, and Klamath; California's contribution was Del Norte´, Siskiyou, Modoc, Humboldt, Trinity, and Shasta.

By Jefferson_state_flag.jpg: Simtropolitan derivative work: Jon C (Jefferson_state_flag.jpg) [Public domain], via Wikimedia Commons

The official seal for the state of Jefferson, and the state flag was a green background with a yellow circle in the center, inside of which were two black XXs. The circle represented a gold pan, and the XXs represented the feeling that the new state felt that it had been "double crossed" by its' respective state governments.

It was decided that prior to obtaining official status that a statewide secession would take place every Thursday, throughout the state of Jefferson. Each Thursday, travelers between Oregon and California were confronted with road blocks, manned with armed, but extremely friendly and polite border guards, who explained the secession movement, and handed out flyers outlining their cause and introducing their new governor. Hollywood camera crews were dispatched to the new state to prepare the newsreels for the media blitz soon to follow.

OREGON

CALIFORNIA

*Jefferson, the 49th state of the United States of America
By User:IMeowbot [Public domain], via Wikimedia Commons
The darker shaded area shows the 1941 proposed State of
Jefferson. Current versions of the still existing movement usually
include the lighter shaded areas.*

Since this was a totally legal secession, it was expected that Congress would approve their statehood, so everything was well on the way to reality for our 49th state. Kickoff for the news releases was set for Monday, December 8, 1941, and was to go national and world wide at the same time. We all know how very close Jefferson came to being! With a war breaking out the day before, there was a bigger cause to support.

Well, we got our roads, and our area became important to the war effort, as the vast stores of copper were of strategic value. Camp White was built and was a huge army post. After World War II, it was disclosed that Camp White had a secret training area that had been designed to replicate the beaches at Normandy, France, and that the troops were trained at this facility for the June 6, 1944 D-Day invasion.

Although we are all one again, when you ask a resident about the state of Jefferson, you can sense a feeling of pride. Not in the fact that there was a secession, but the pride of a people that have a certain independence in their lives to this day. People who move here soon feel the independence and quickly assimilate. Welcome to the state of Jefferson.

WHERE DOES THE SASQUATCH GO TO DIE?

Why are the remains of these giant creatures never found? With all of the sightings and encounters why has no one ever found a body?

This question has been nagging us ever since we had our first sighting and began our interviews with all of the contributors to our books. One highly respected theorist and Sasquatch expert is Dr. Donald Jeffrey Meldrum, professor of anatomy and anthropology at Idaho State University. Dr. Meldrum has theorized that the Sasquatch is an extremely solitary being, and as such, he says the creature, "Goes off to a very remote place to die." The doctor has an extensive collection of Bigfoot footprint casts, hair samples, and a vast knowledge of this mysterious creature.

We received an alternative explanation from another doctor, who we're going to refer to as "Dr. Sam," to protect her identity. She is also a highly respected educator, but she admits to only recently completing a three year research project into the Bigfoot as a personal interest project and unsponsored by her university. Her theory may shed further light on another lingering question; however we make no attempt to disclose any of her findings, opinions or research.

Dr. Sam's research has attempted to answer the often asked

question of, "What about the Sasquatch that dies from other than a peaceful death?" What if one fell off of a cliff, was killed by a falling rock, a sudden flash flood, shot by a hunter, or an endless list of reasons? In these cases, if this solitary creature dies, why then does no one, including humans, dogs and other animals ever find its remains? All carnivorous animals will leave remains; such as fur, claws, skull, skeleton, etc. Even vultures leave some skeletal remains as they ravage a cadaver. We have tons of information about dinosaurs, but so little of Sasquatch!

Expounding on Dr. Sam's research, I look back at my first exposure to the mysterious Sasquatch creature. Thirty years before Wendy and I met, I remember hearing about Bigfoot experiences from people in Minnesota, Wisconsin, Michigan, Illinois, Montana, South Dakota and Idaho, and I assumed that these stories were too far-fetched to be true even though they were all so similar; I missed the obvious validation. As time went on and the reports continued, it gave me cause to simply accept the reports "with a grain of salt." My first really believable story came from people I was doing business with in Washington state. I had relocated to Oregon and was conducting a transaction with a family in Washington when they breached the subject of Bigfoot.

After Wendy and I had become interested in publishing these Sasquatch encounters, I touched on the story from this family, but I only reported a part of it due to the fact that I had doubts about the validity. I have since learned enough more from the experiences of dozens of other people that I will report the entire story that, along with ideas from Dr. Sam, may help explain where the Sasquatch goes to die.

As I looked back on this story and my judgement that the end lacked credibility, I had to ask myself, "Who makes me the expert?" So now after first hearing this experience 46 years ago and very similar ones so many times since, I have changed my thinking and I am more open to Dr. Sam's theory. We anticipate the entire theory to be forthcoming after she has completed further studies that are ongoing at this time

I now think back to a story told me in about 1971 when I was working with this couple from the state of Washington. These folks were both in their fifties; the gentleman was a professor at a major university and his wife was a president at a nearby college. Their teenage sons were honor students, and this affluent family lived in a beautiful home with endless acreage in forests and a small, private lake; it was an all-around beautiful property. The parents described their home to me and showed me photos as we talked.

After we had shaken hands on a deal and were awaiting my people to prepare the paperwork, they told me about an experience they had with Sasquatch. I had of course heard of this being in other states, but never before had I met anyone who actually saw one.

As they told me about their experiences, I was fascinated! Not only had they seen one, they had met it face to face and had followed a small one a few days later to a secluded valley on their property. I grew intrigued by their experiences over what had occurred over about a years' time, and then they invited me to have dinner at their home, saying they and their boys would take me back on their property and show me the signs that were in the Bigfoot's "hideout." I gladly accepted, and then my business manager was ready to do their paperwork so we agreed to talk after the transaction was concluded.

Before they left to return home they took me aside, saying there was more to the story; they said I needed to prepare for my visit by wearing older clothes and boots for the walk, and then they told me the rest of the story; that's when I went from *excited believer* to *disappointed!*

They told me that they had saved this last part because they had experienced a change of attitude with some close friends when they related this part of the story and didn't want to lay it all on me at once because, "It is too hard for most people to comprehend." They said they felt I had the intelligence to accept the rest of it. That's where they were wrong! I wasn't that smart evidently, because what they told me next left me nodding and feigning excitement, but inside I was totally dismayed. Looking back now after all these years, I think I missed a great opportunity. I could have seen for myself the proof that we keep searching for today!

What they went on to tell me was too much for my doubting mind to comprehend. Going through the motions, I listened as intently as I could when they told me that the night after their first encounter with the adult Sasquatch, they saw what appeared to be bright lights like a fire in the higher meadow behind their house. The next morning was a Saturday, so they trekked up through the forest to the large mountain meadow and there was a huge burned circle. All of the grass and bushes had been scorched right down to the dirt. Then they said two nights later they were in the yard having a late barbeque when a large saucer shaped object came over the nearest mountain and hovered over the same pasture. What they described was a flying saucer that had strange lights (they called them landing lights) that lit up the ground directly underneath the craft so bright it could have been a circus event.

They went on to tell me that they had seen it land one more time a week or so later, but over the last month they had not seen it again, nor had they seen the creatures again, but the signs were still visible and they looked forward to showing me. We agreed that we would check our calendars and I'd get back to them to set a date for dinner and "Sasquatch hunting," but this last part of their story had taken me all the way from a fascinated and enthusiastic believer to a disappointed skeptic.

I truthfully experienced a huge letdown! From super excitement to utter disappointment, like finding out there really is no Santa Claus. So I did the worst thing I could do; I purposely did not return their phone calls, they made three; I'm sure they were dismayed, but I was so thoroughly convinced that they were crazy that I lost all common sense. Certainly this highly educated, wealthy and successful family did not get where they were by being "kooky." I obviously had not thought it all the way through.

Now, here I am 46 years later and having heard of so many instances where our submitters have seen both Sasquatch and some sort of spacecraft closely around that same time, I wonder; could it be somehow significant?

It makes one speculate if the reason that a deceased Sasquatch has never truly been identified is because an extraterrestrial craft takes them away. Many of our submitters have implied that they believed there to be a tie-in between the Bigfoot sightings and the strange aerial lights along with burned areas on the ground that may indicate the comings and goings of this animal. Could it mean that these strange creatures exist on another planet somewhere and maybe they are simply coming and going to learn about us? Although Dr. Sam has not expounded on this theory, she has mentioned it as worthy of further consideration and we anxiously await her release when her conclusions are finalized.

One submitter, who has lived for years off the grid, gave us some information by a story penned for him by the owner of a remote country store, because the man could not read or write. A friend had told him of our books and our inquiries in the area and the gentleman wanted his story told, so he enlisted the help of the store owner he bought his supplies from. The store owner has been a true friend, both to our write and to us as well!

Our storyteller had inherited a gold claim from his brother and has spent the majority of his life in an extremely remote area of Oregon, and he claims to have seen and observed the Bigfoot comings and goings. He even has had occasions where he harvested deer and hung out some cuts of meat away from his camp as a token of friendship to these "mountain apes," as he calls them, and actually saw a Sasquatch take his offerings on several occasions and then furtively depart for the remote canyon that he believed it lived in. Once, after being away from his cabin for a couple of days he came home to find a large piece of curved tree bark full of blackberries sitting by his door. One could conclude this was an attempt on the Bigfoot's part to communicate by paying back a gift of food.

Since, as he explained, his cabin is actually a boarded up front door to his mine as well as his living quarters, they seldom come close when he's working and he figures they are afraid of the mining and the occasional charge of dynamite he has used. Such a lonely existence with only a simple window looking outside and a second door just fifteen feet away to a dark, damp hole in the cliff, I could imagine having any creature for a friend would be welcome.

Thanks to the storekeeper, who wishes to remain anonymous, for exchanging the information for us and agreeing to read aloud the book we delivered for our miner friend. We hope he enjoyed hearing that he is not alone in his experiences.

Another item of interest is that on two separate occasions about six months apart, our mine owner said he had observed bright lights back above the remote part of the canyon, and at both times, he saw one of the mountain apes. The significance of these two events were that after each of these lighting occurrences he saw the Sasquatch several days in a row and then no more for months to come. It was funny the way he put it, because he said, "It was like a shift change when I worked for the mill; the excitement of all the lights coming on and a lot of hustle and bustle and then a new face!"

The reason he remarked on it was because the first creature was quite a bit smaller and lighter colored, but the second one was much bigger and with longer, darker fur. It also walked like it had more authority; he called it "Boss Man."

This is another of many observations which we have had reported to us since we rather skeptically began collecting these stories until we gradually became believers in not only the likelihood that these beings exist, but in the fact that they may have an agenda. Perhaps it is a special purpose to just not observe and learn, but with some other and possibly more important reason for visiting our world? This opinion is not mine, but it has been suggested on occasion by several of our contributors.

As a final note, I need to say that Dr. Sam's field of expertise is not even remotely connected in any relation to our research; she is undertaking further studies of the Bigfoot as both a serious endeavor and a hobby. We thank her for sharing and appreciate her input.

Gary Swanson ~ Southern Utah

ABOUT THE AUTHORS

Gary and Wendy Swanson have recently located to Southern Utah, but lived in Grants Pass, Oregon for the last eight years, where they enjoyed hiking throughout the spring, summer and fall months with their dogs. In addition to their love of hiking, they also enjoy history. Southern Oregon is full of history of gold mining, logging and fishing along the wild and scenic Rogue River; so for them, it has been a great place to research history, explore the countryside and hike all at the same time. Their attention gradually was drawn to the many people they met who had sighted and encountered the Sasquatch. Along with their own experiences, they began to collect stories from others. They are still in constant contact with people throughout Oregon as they continue researching and report the Bigfoot stories that keep coming in.